1986

Ethics, Deterrence, and National Security

James E. Dougherty
Midge Decter
Pierre Hassner
Laurence Martin
Michael Novak
Vladimir Bukovsky

Foreign Policy Report
June 1985

Published in cooperation with the
INSTITUTE FOR FOREIGN POLICY ANALYSIS, INC.

 PERGAMON·BRASSEY'S
International Defense Publishers

Washington New York Oxford Toronto Sydney Paris Frankfurt

Pergamon Press Offices:

U.S.A.	Pergamon-Brassey's International Defense Publishers, 1340 Old Chain Bridge Road, McLean, Virginia, 22101, U.S.A.
	Pergamon Press Inc., Maxwell House, Fairview Park, Elmsford, New York 10523, U.S.A.
U.K.	Pergamon Press Ltd., Headington Hill Hall, Oxford OX3 0BW, England
CANADA	Pergamon Press Canada Ltd., Suite 104, 150 Consumers Road, Willowdale, Ontario M2J 1P9, Canada
AUSTRALIA	Pergamon Press (Aust.) Pty. Ltd., P.O. Box 544, Potts Point, NSW 2011, Australia
FRANCE	Pergamon Press SARL, 24 rue des Ecoles, 75240 Paris, Cedex 05, France
FEDERAL REPUBLIC OF GERMANY	Pergamon Press GmbH, Hammerweg 6, D-6242 Kronberg-Taunus, Federal Republic of Germany

Copyright © 1985 Institute for Foreign Policy Analysis, Inc.

Library of Congress Cataloging in Publication Data
Main entry under title:

Ethics, deterrence, and national security.

(Foreign policy report)
Conference held June 23-25, 1983 in Bonn, Germany
by the Institute for Foreign Policy Analysis and the
Konrad Adenauer Foundation.
    1. Nuclear warfare--Moral and ethical aspects--
Congresses. 2. Deterrence (Strategy)--Moral and
ethical aspects--Congresses. 3. Just war doctrine--
Congresses. 4. Europe--Defenses--Moral and ethical
aspects--Congresses. I. Dougherty, James E.
II. Institute for Foreign Policy Analysis.
III. Konrad-Adenauer-Stiftung. IV. Series.
U263.E83   1985   172'.42   85-3699
ISBN 0-08-032767-2 (pbk.)

Printed in the United States of America

Contents

Preface

Between June 23 and 25, 1983, the Institute for Foreign Policy Analysis, with the Konrad Adenauer Foundation, convened in Bonn a Conference whose purpose was to address the fundamental issues raised by the various antinuclear movements in Western Europe and their implications for transatlantic security. The Conference represented a logical extension of other meetings held by both sponsoring organizations on security issues of importance to the Federal Republic of Germany and the United States. These have included the German-American Roundtable conferences, whose focus has been political-military issues within the context of the Atlantic Alliance, and a series of meetings, with Japanese participation and co-sponsorship, on the future of nuclear energy held sequentially in the United States, the Federal Republic of Germany, and Japan.

Because of the importance of the public debate on defense policy and the role of nuclear weapons in Western strategies to deter, or prevent, the outbreak of armed conflict, the organizers of the Conference brought together a distinguished group of participants from diverse professional backgrounds and perspectives, from Western Europe and the United States. The Conference furnished an opportunity to examine the origins and tactics of the antinuclear movement, as well as the dilemmas posed by nuclear weapons for traditional conceptions of "just war," the ethical considerations associated with deterrence, and the utilization by the Soviet Union of "peace" as a political weapon. In keeping with the transatlantic focus of the Conference, there was substantial consideration of the antinuclear campaign, including the nuclear freeze movement, in the United States, as well as the Pastoral Letter of the American Catholic Bishops.

This Foreign Policy Report contains updated and revised versions of several papers presented at the Conference as the basis for the discussions that took place. They are published in this format in order to give broader dissemination to the issues and themes that were addressed at the Conference. This Foreign Policy Report forms part of a series of Institute studies designed to assess the implications of the breakdown in several NATO countries of the domestic and political consensus that has sustained the security policies upon which the Atlantic Alliance has been based.

Special thanks are extended to the United States Information Agency and the John M. Olin Foundation for grants to the Institute for Foreign Policy Analysis that helped to make possible the organizing and convening of this conference.

Robert L. Pfaltzgraff, Jr.
President
Institute for Foreign Policy Analysis, Inc.

Summary Overview

Religious/Philosophical Roots of the Peace Movement

West Europeans harbored misgivings about nuclear weapons and strategies long before the INF (intermediate nuclear force) debate began. They worried about "Finlandization," the credibility of the U.S. deterrent in the face of a massive Soviet military buildup, and uncertainty concerning the steadfastness of American leadership and policies. Government policymakers and strategic analysts who originally had welcomed the presence of U.S. tactical nuclear weapons as pillars of deterrence when the United States enjoyed strategic superiority began to doubt their utility and even to express fears of "decoupling" after the codification of strategic nuclear parity in SALT I. They were unenthusiastic, however, about U.S. pressure upon the NATO allies to upgrade conventional capabilities. They generally prefer war-deterrence over war-fighting strategies, and they know that nuclear deterrence is much cheaper and more effective than conventional deterrence. Some may have quietly appreciated the "peace movement" as an excuse for holding off INF deployments as long as possible while seeking an arms agreement with the USSR at Geneva. The fragility and thin parliamentary margins of governing parties and coalitions in several West European countries in the 1979-1981 period often dictated ambiguity in foreign and defense policy while the antinuclear protest demonstrations were growing.

The outpouring of emotions, zeal, passionate righteousness, and crusading spirit known as "the peace movement" may be utopian in its goals but it has been quite shrewd in its methods. The term itself is a misnomer, for it implies a monopoly of virtuous dedication to peace. Political pacifism has never been known to head off a war, but it did help to bring one on in the late 1930s. The protest movement is by no means monolithic. It varies from country to country and is made up of different elements—political party factions, women's organizations, ecological and pacifist societies, and most countercultural groups. Since all of these have their own agenda, they are bound to disagree over principles, goals, and tactics. Superficial media pundits have invested it with a unity it does not possess.

Much of the movement's success has resulted from deftly playing upon themes deeply rooted in European thought. The first is Marxist-Leninist socialism, which equates the "capitalist West" with ruthless exploitation of the world's poor and with preparations for war. This is not to suggest that the "peace movement" is purely and simply a Soviet export, despite the key role played by the Moscow-directed World Peace Council. The movement has an indigenous base in the Western psyche which the communists deftly exploit. Decades of Pavlovian conditioning have made Western intellectuals and opinion-molders more likely to give the benefit of the doubt to the Soviet leadership than to their own governments.

The peace movement knows better what it opposes than what it is for. Nuclear weapons are looked upon by many as the key symbol of the Western capitalist-industrial-imperial culture, the ultimate absurd product of Enlightenment rationalist science, with all that faith in democracy, technology, and progress which the early 19th century European Romantics came to despise. The new romantic antinuclearists oppose all modern offspring of the Enlightenment—parliamentary government, bureaucracy, science, technology, industrialization, and commerce. When it comes to nuclear weapons, they reject as irrelevant all arguments based on technical, strategic, or political considerations. Nothing counts except feeling, intuition, and deep spiritual revulsion against contemporary economic development—a fact which gives rise to confusion among the romantic conservers of nature, since Marxists also exploit nature and technology to the hilt and show even less concern for the environment than Western societies. In Germany and elsewhere in the West, the gnawing unease over the direction of social evolution and the dissolution of traditional values produced widespread alienation, cultural pessimism, and *angst*.

Existentialists, whether Christian or atheist, view man as alienated and destined for unrelieved suffering, tragedy, ambiguity, and contradiction on earth despite his quest for happiness. Existentialist ideas, therefore, stand in negative critique of ideological pacifists who hope to escape from *angst*. But they support the peace movement's conviction that Western civilization is not worth defending at the potential cost of nuclear war and that the rational decision-making processes on which the theory of deterrence rests is bound to break down under the strains of a future crisis.

The "Ecopeace" movement, resenting the consumerism of capitalist, industrial society, is against the pollution of the environment, against bigness in all forms, and against military alliances and the division of Europe. It protests more against the nuclear weapons which defend Western Europe than those which target it. In Germany, it has become infused with the leftist neo-nationalism of the Greens—an antiparliamentary party which, along with the left wing of the SPD, would seek national reunification through demilitarization and neutralism.

In the Netherlands, Britain, West Germany, and elsewhere, the Christian Churches have lent social respectability and large numbers of middle-class recruits to the antinuclear campaign. There was a strong intellectual sentiment in favor of pacifism in the first three centuries of Church history. But ever since Christians began to assume responsibility for preserving social order in the fourth century, the Church has preached the doctrine of the "just war," waged for a rightful cause and in a limited, discriminating manner. Christians have faced an increasingly agonizing moral dilemma with regard to the justification of modern technological warfare, even prior to the appearance of nuclear weapons. During the last two decades, several factors, including political and liberation theology and the Vietnam War, have produced a larger segment of radicalized Christian clergy, the growth of nuclear pacifism, and the transmutation of the doctrine of the just war into a doctrine of justified revolutionary violence in "wars of national liberation" in the Third World. The Catholic Church, especially Pope John Paul II, has adhered to teaching the just war doctrine and has regarded nuclear deterrence as morally acceptable under present circumstances, whereas the World Council of Churches, meeting in August 1983 at Vancouver, called nuclear deterrence a "crime against humanity." French and West German Catholic bishops, who live in the zone of initial encounter as potential victims of aggression, are much less ready than their fellow bishops in the United States to renounce the first use of nuclear weapons as a part of NATO strategy.

Democratic Ideals, Democratic Realities

During recent decades, ideals have become distorted and debased. We have watched privileged youths and adults in Western Europe and North America, living in societies that provided wealth, ease, and a full range of private choices, attack their own societies and institutions as offering only an imperfect mortal existence. Life proved to be full of obligations, difficult choices, and moral necessities. So, in the name of idealism, they rebelled against that world and chose evasion, narcissism, drugs, infantile leftism, and often suicide.

There may be no greater truth for our time than that contained in the old adage: The perfect is the enemy of the good. Seeking the perfect has long provided a handy antidote to the need to make serious moral choices, as in the question: Since Western society is wanting in this or that respect, why should we differentiate it from Soviet society? To be idealistic and utopian, then, is to do away with the need to be moral.

Politicians who wish to appear as feeling and sensitive refer to the "peace movement" as being made up of decent people, motivated by the highest ideals. The truth is that these people are idealists, which is to say, moral evaders, who are looking for a quick fix in a situation that offers none—looking for the unattainable because it feels more pleasing to do so, and damn the consequences. Being idealistic is anything but noble and, in truth, far from decent.

We should set aside our careless impulse to speak of democratic ideals and concentrate instead on democratic realities. Soviet communism has, since its rise to power in Russia, been an expansive, aggressive force, seeking by subversion, by intimidation, in recent decades by nuclear blackmail, and, where necessary or possible, by outright military conquest, to achieve hegemony over the world. The only thing that has stood between the Soviet Union and the realization of its international ambitions has been the alliance headed by the United States and supported by the nations of Western Europe and Japan.

That alliance now seems to be coming unstuck. The West Europeans, not without a great deal of justice, have lost faith in the capacity of the United States to play the role history has handed it; the Americans, with equal justice, have lost faith in the West Europeans' commitment to bearing their rightful share of the common burden.

The precious gift we call Western democracy is indivisible: Should Western Europe go down, by surrender or by defeat in battle, so too would the United States—and vice versa. What sustains our societies is not only the safeguarding of our respective national interests but our common political, social, and moral ethos. A major blow to that ethos on either side of the Atlantic will have dire consequences for the other side.

We are threatened not, as the idealists in the West have been declaring, primarily with the extinction of the planet, but with the collapse of our finely wrought and delicately balanced plural societies beneath the weight of the ponderous barbarism called communism. No one any longer should harbor illusions about communism. No matter how ugly or cruel the government replaced by it, communist regimes have created even greater misery: more poverty, oppression, despair, murder, and aggression. On the other side are modern Western societies whose discovery of the principle of liberty has provided their citizens with freedom, both public and private, and with the means to create undreamed of wealth and to distribute that wealth more broadly, more equitably, than any other society in human history.

Controlling the Arms Race: Can We Deal with the Totalitarians?

Notwithstanding Max Weber's observation—"With the champions of faith, no dialogue is possible"—a potential does exist, even among ideological foes, for rational communication based on common interests. The real question concerning arms control is whether it is realistic, or whether the primacy of political conflict and the influence of strategic constraints make it a dangerous illusion.

The primacy of politics dictates an arms control policy that steers between total unilateral disarmament and total military victory through unrestrained warfare. Are self-restraint and reciprocity possible between the superpowers? Before we can answer that, we must reveal the assumptions underlying our conceptions of morality, arms control, military technology, and political strategy.

Political communities are based on certain unspoken assumptions which citizens are not supposed to question. Yet our Judeo-Christian moral tradition compels the individual conscience to take stands and, at times, to make radical moral choices. The American Catholic Bishops reject the threat of countercity retaliation, strongly doubt the possibility of keeping nuclear war limited, and distinguish between the mere possession of nuclear weapons and the threat to use them. Their first position is unassailable; the second is empirically arguable; the third is debatable on theological, psychological, and political grounds as erosive of deterrence.

The problem is much more complex than the simple "Red or dead" dichotomy. Is the killing of millions or tens of millions in defense or retaliation morally worse than holding hundreds of millions hostage? Karl Jaspers stated our dilemma in terms of the twin dangers: nuclear weapons which destroy life, or totalitarianism which deprives life of value. We cannot rest contented merely with setting the ethics of conviction against the ethics of responsibility. The two must be combined. The responsible man may have to take an absolute moral stand, and the moral purist cannot ignore consequences. The essence of the problem is to prevent from ever arising the extreme situation that demands the ultimate, absolute, radical moral choice. Leo Strauss believes that the true statesman takes his bearings from what is normally right, and deviates from this course only to save justice and humanity itself. It is up to the historian later to judge whether he acted rightly or not. Karl Jaspers thinks in terms of an existential gamble from which the elements of freedom and uncertainty cannot be entirely eliminated, not even in the historian's retrospect. One, however, cannot take the ultimate decision for the extreme situation in the normal present.

Can we deal with the totalitarians? This involves both firmness and openness. In religious terms, we must love our enemies; we need not forget that they are enemies. A real peace ethic cannot consider weapons only. It must recognize existing asymmetries in political regimes and seek to move from minimal reciprocity based on mutual interest in survival to a genuine reciprocity based on political reconciliation. Rational arms control policy requires discrimination among populations, military forces, and leaders; and the avoidance of nuclear escalation, nuclear retaliation against cities, "launch on warning," and any posture which makes early use of nuclear weapons inevitable. It calls for limited counterforce nuclear options—strategies of mutual assured survival rather than destruction, i.e., the coupling of anti-missile defense with reductions in offensive weapons. The arms control dialogue should promote constructive communication without implying a quest for agreement merely for agreement's sake. We must expect that cooperation in the search for common rules will continue to be mixed with conflict between systems.

Technological progress in precision and control of weapons will enhance our freedom to choose proportionally restrained responses. Enhanced radiation weapons constitute a positive step toward resolving our dilemma. But such issues as the limitability of nuclear war and the feasibility of "star wars" defense are clouded by uncertainty. Is the risk of escalation to mutual suicide the ultimate foundation of peace? We loathe that idea, yet we cannot entirely disengage from it. The effort to develop a more credible, stable deterrent based on damage-limitation is equally endangered by advocates of a nuclear freeze and by those who, in their zeal for sophisticated new technologies, may facilitate an easier resort to limited nuclear war. A world of invulnerable weapons and vulnerable populations is a mad world. Not all new technologies are inherently destabilizing—some should be discouraged, some encouraged. We have no choice but to keep steering between opposite dangers.

Managing the dilemmas of morality and arms control, of maintaining credible deterrence and an operational damage-limiting defense if deterrence should fail, is the highest task of politics. The current debate about Pershing and cruise missiles is not really about nuclear war. It is a political struggle for the soul of the Europeans, especially the Germans, and the future political fate of the Continent. France understands this, and thus has no real pacifist movement. Because the United States does not understand it, and insists upon casting the argument in military terms, it has frightened its own population and even more that of the European allies. Deterrence should be rational, credible and correspond to what one actually intends to do if it fails. We must reconcile deterrence, reassurance to all of our people, and defense, while trying to be faithful to the moral imperative of desperately trying to preserve the normal and humane without absolutely excluding the extreme. We need an ability to communicate moderation and resolve, the sense of responsibility that goes with freedom, and the feeling of awe before the destructive force waiting to be unleashed.

Nuclear Deterrence, Statesmanship, and Ethics

The notion of deterrence is old—"*si vis pacem* . . . "—but nuclear deterrence is an entirely new concept because of the dire consequences of its failure and the lack of an alternative in an effective strategy of defense. Early nuclear deterrent strategies focused on "city-busting" retaliatory threats, although interest in military targets was never abandoned. McNamara's doctrine of assured destruction, designed to destroy the Soviet Union "as a twentieth century society," aims at the promotion of stability, but it contains flaws: it perpetuates the possibility of mutual catastrophe, breeds proposals for "star wars" defense, and makes the world seem safe once again for large-scale conventional wars which may nevertheless escalate to the nuclear level. Many antinuclearists, including not a few bishops, hope to enjoy the continued deterrent effect of nuclear weapons while professing the view that they must never be used. They rest their hopes on a wasting asset, which their own declarations help to erode.

The supreme task is to prevent nuclear war from occurring, not to avoid all personal implication in the use of nuclear weapons. This is a matter of politics and strategy. Pacifism may destroy alliances which restrain nuclear proliferation, or encourage blackmail and aggression. Deterrence is the least destructive strategy of all so long as it is successful. It may fail, but so may all other approaches. We should do our utmost to make deterrence succeed and, if it fails, to keep the war as limited, proportionate and discriminating as possible. Even if nuclear deterrence can be justified, it should not be over-burdened; it must be supplemented by conventional defense and diplomacy aimed at mitigating international conflict. Responsible statesmanship will avoid needlessly provocative or destabilizing postures.

Christian and humanist thought in the West has evolved the doctrine of the "just war" which requires the observance of due proportion, not on-ly with regard to the cause for going to war (*jus ad bellum*) but also, and more controversially, in the conduct of the war itself (*jus in bello*). Moreover, the principle of discrimination demanded sparing the lives of innocent non-combatants. Whether the doctrine is or is not valid ethics, it has never been good history. As for deterrence, most would agree that an assured destruc-tion strike, and even a substantial counterforce strike, would fail to meet the conditions laid down in the "just war" doctrine.

Some would escape the moral dilemma by adopting nuclear pacifism, but this would leave the worst weapons in the worst hands, to be used for war or blackmail. Solzhenitsyn has said that it could not be better to be Red than dead because to be Red was to be dead. The pacifist can renounce freedom for self but cannot impose that choice upon others. Nor can we solve the problem easily by shifting to conventional defense which, though extremely expensive, furnishes no guarantee against nuclear blackmail or defeat in a destructive war, whether conventional or nuclear. Not even multilateral nuclear disarmament would provide full security against future nuclear war. Those who advocate limited nuclear warfare strategies always come up against the specter of uncontrollable escalation.

NATO retains the option of using nuclear weapons first in response to prior aggression, thereby shifting the onus to the attacker. Deterrence can-not be a mere bluff or sham, for that may combine dangerous provocation with ineffectiveness.

The Morality of Strategic Deterrence

Western public opinion concerning nuclear weapons has undergone a fundamental change in the last decade because the Soviet Union has gone beyond strategic nuclear parity with the West, has achieved virtual parity in quality with NATO conventional arms while maintaining a wide quan-titative edge, and since 1977 has targeted Western Europe with SS-20s. These changes have induced a considerable and appropriate fear in Europe that the once protective U.S. nuclear umbrella has collapsed, and some observers are arguing that American troops in Europe now expose the United States to nuclear blackmail and may soon have to be withdrawn. As a result of the new fear and confusion, four different perceptions of the situation are now widely held in Western Europe: (1) Since the superpowers pose relatively equal threats to European security, neutralism is the way to peace. (2) The USSR is not aggressive, but paranoid. (3) The Reagan Administration has overestimated, and is over-responding to, the Soviet threat. (4) The Soviet threat is real, and Soviet power is dangerous, but there is disagreement over the proper response.

We must distinguish among Soviet intentions, proclivities, and strategic potential, always keeping the "worst case" possibility in mind. Given his assets, what range of options is open to the opponent? Proclivities, reflected in well-established patterns of behavior, based on historical, cultural, psychological, ideological, and geopolitical factors, are more knowable than intentions. Leninist doctrine, which mandates cool judgment about the probabilities of success and failure, tilts the leadership toward caution.

The Europeans, being closer to the threat, may be better analysts of the Soviet Union than Americans are, but they face special spiritual temptations, because they have experienced two world wars in this century. Some of them are probably angry with the United States for having allowed the USSR to pierce the protective nuclear shield. Capitalist and social democratic societies do not cultivate martial virtues; they instill a due regard for small gains and losses, as well as prudent compromise—which is not the stuff of heroism. Democratic peoples are not easily aroused to wars and crusades. Pluralistic societies reject the traditional notion of unquestioned loyalty to the state, and prize criticism of the state by universities, media, and other groups. Thus, the states which comprise NATO may appear to be no less spiritually empty than those of the East. But the appearance is deceptive. The prudence of our middle-aged political and economic leaderships falls between the idealism of the young and the wisdom of the aged.

Three of the four putative functions of nuclear weapons do not require their actual use. The chief moral imperative of our age is to prevent both the unjust military use of nuclear weapons in war and the unjust use of such weapons for purposes of intimidation. Some moralists would wash their hands of moral responsibility by saying that it is permissible to *possess* nuclear weapons but wrong in any way to *use* them or to *intend* to use them in military combat. This is moral casuistry of the worst sort, no less hypocritical than the position of Pilate.

The possession of nuclear weapons necessarily includes intentions. A deterrent is an intentional process which must always be held at the ready. If it has no intention and makes no threat, it is empty. Without a will to inflict punishment, the deterrent becomes like the ceremonial pikestaffs of the Swiss Guards in the Vatican. Those who question the morality of deterrence are concerned about its *breakdown*. The greatest moral danger lies in eroding the adequacy and credibility of the deterrent threat, the maintenance of which requires high moral courage and nobility of soul.

Given the Soviet proclivity to probe weakness, those who would try to buy deterrence "on the cheap" bear a tragic moral responsibility. Against the argument that the effort to keep the deterrent credible leads inexorably to costly new spirals in the "arms race," it must be remembered that conventional deterrence could be as much as nine times more expensive. From 1970 to 1983, spending on nuclear weapons constituted only 8 percent of the military budget. Generational modernization has made the deterrent more effective, more moral in terms of proportionality and discrimination, and more strictly defensive. Indeed, if President Reagan's defensive shield is technically feasible, it should be pursued. World government, a nuclear freeze, pre-emptive surrender, and passive resistance are not viable alternatives to deterrence. What the West now needs to defend are not higher spiritual values, but the political institutions which alone make the practice and preservation of those values possible.

The "Struggle for Peace": Soviet Foreign Policy Tool

The Western "peace movement," while not a communist conspiracy, has certainly been manipulated by the Soviet Union. The "struggle for peace" has always been a useful tool of Soviet foreign policy. Communists invariably present themselves as "peace-lovers," all the more so now when they are striving to retain their nuclear superiority, silence criticism of their adventurism in the Third World and of their domestic human rights violations, and increase their influence in a pacified Western Europe.

The overwhelming majority of adherents to the peace movement are well-intentioned but confused, naive, and frightened people who have been exploited by a handful of agitators directed from Moscow. Thus, they vented their spleen against the Americans, but avoided condemning Soviet imperialism in Afghanistan and Poland. They take their signals from Moscow, never from Washington. Communists are represented in the leadership out of all proportion to their numbers in the rank-and-file of peace groups. Moscow coins the slogans which show up from one to six months later in Western Europe.

The Soviet Union decided to activate its "struggle for peace" in the summer of 1979, while deploying SS-20s at the rate of one per week and planning military intervention in Afghanistan. The decision was made public during the "World Parliament of Peoples for Peace," held at Sofia, Bulgaria, and attended by delegates from 137 countries in September 1980. A month later, huge peace demonstrations began in West European capitals. The Sofia gathering was organized not by the Soviet government or by the Party, but by the front organization known as the World Peace Council.

The Soviet master brainwashers are adept at confronting human beings with "absolute values"—such as rejecting global nuclear destruction. This eliminates the anguish of having to choose, but it also enslaves. The American Catholic bishops, who should be more concerned with a man's soul than with his survival, should have been more wary of the Soviet propaganda trap. But who cares how many people may be arrested, tortured, or killed by the Soviets or how many new missiles Moscow is deploying, when it is humanity itself that we must save from destruction? In order to work for survival, we must all unite, irrespective of political differences and past crimes. Moscow does not attempt to conceal its efforts to direct the peace movements, and to assist them with financial aid, trips to the USSR, conferences, advice, and other forms of support.

The peace movement began to undergo some changes not to Soviet liking in the early 1980s. Stung by criticisms that it was too one-sided, some of its leaders felt compelled to adopt more balanced positions, and the movement started to split into pro-Soviet and more impartial elements. Spirits within the peace movement dampened after the Soviet-inspired clampdown on Polish Solidarity. After the American "zero-option" proposal in November 1981, Moscow began to appear more intransigent. Finally, the USSR began to persecute independent peace movements in the Eastern camp. Moscow clearly understands the danger to its position in Europe if it loses control over the peace movement in the West and faces a rising protest movement in the East.

The West has shown in the Geneva arms negotiations that it does not fully understand the significance and possibilities of the evolving situation. Instead of concentrating on arms control reduction talks, Western statesmen should urge the convening of a conference to negotiate the postwar treaty in Europe which still does not exist. This would allow us to focus on the real issues—i.e., the illegitimate Soviet empire in Eastern Europe—and throw the Soviet Union onto the defensive in the face of rising resentment on the part of many subjugated nationalities. Then it will be the Soviet Union that will be blamed for perpetuating international tensions, and the crowds will shift to the Western side. If the West misses its opportunity, it will deserve nothing better than a futile, endless arms race and creeping Soviet expansion.

Contemporary Religious/Philosophical Thought and the Peace Movement in Western Europe

by James E. Dougherty*

MORE THAN two decades ago, in the late 1950s and early 1960s, the peoples of Western Europe were quite content to see a strategically superior United States deploy tactical nuclear weapons on their soil. Even though most of those weapons were of short range, it was assumed that their presence strengthened the effectiveness of a deterrent strategy which was highly credible at the time. It seems odd now to remember that the Dutch, of all people, were the first to welcome those weapons on their territory. Since then, opinion in Western Europe has changed significantly, along with the global and regional "correlation of forces."

We should not forget, of course, that there were sizeable though short-lived protests in West Germany—the "Gottingen Appeal" in the spring of 1957 and the "Kampf dem Atomtod" which brought out hundreds of thousands of demonstrators for several months in 1958—against the decision to arm the Bundeswehr with nuclear-capable delivery systems. But those protests were largely of a partisan political nature, and arose out of the differing view of Christian Democrats and Social Democrats concerning the best course to be pursued by West Germany in the long run—close political, economic and military integration with Western Europe and the Atlantic Community or demilitarization and neutrality—with particular reference to the eventual goal of some kind of national reunification.[1] Only since the late 1970s, beginning with the remarkably successful campaign of the Netherlands' Inter-Church Peace Council (IKV) to gather a million signatures against the deployment of U.S. neutron weapons in Europe, has the issue of nuclear weapons begun to catch on widely as the focus of a more comprehensive countercultural movement.

The Growth of Antinuclearism and Pacifism

One can cite several pragmatic reasons for the growth of antinuclearism and pacifism in Western Europe during recent years. For two decades, a

---

* The author is indebted to James B. Foley and Clay Clemens for their assistance in the research and analysis that went into the preparation of this paper.
[1] See Jeffrey Boutwell, "Politics and the Peace Movement in West Germany," *International Security*, Spring 1983, esp. pp. 72-77.

1

parade of personages from de Gaulle to Kissinger plus a bevy of less distinguished commentators had been casting doubt upon the reliability of the U.S. pledge to come to the defense of Europe with nuclear weapons. From the signing of SALT I onward, strategists on both sides of the Atlantic had been concerned over the implications of a codified strategic parity between the superpowers for the regional military balance. All through the years of a tortuous debate about "massive retaliation," "flexible response," "forward strategy," the "conventional pause" and the "rules of engagement" within NATO, many Europeans could not decide which was more worrisome—that the United States might someday defend them, or that it would not defend them.

Throughout the 1970s, the Soviet Union carried on a buildup of strategic and regional forces, both nuclear and conventional, at a steady and disquieting rate. There was increasing talk that Western Europe might see its defense "decoupled" from that of the United States (itself more inward-looking after the trauma of Vietnam) and undergo a process of "Finlandization"—implying some kind of subtle intimidation which would compel several capitals to emulate Helsinki by reorienting their political compasses toward the new global gravity center in Moscow. For several years the United States had sought to persuade its NATO allies to strengthen their conventional capabilities, but the NATO decision in the Carter years to increase defense spending by 3 percent per year in real terms (after inflation) met with only limited and ephemeral success for understandable reasons: the Europeans have always believed in war-deterrence rather than war-fighting strategies; they are convinced that nuclear deterrence is much cheaper and much more effective than conventional deterrence; and they were unwilling in a period of low economic growth rates and high inflation/unemployment rates to shift from a superior but cheap strategy to an inferior but expensive one.

European uncertainties about the quality of U.S. political leadership became more acute in the late 1970s. When Chancellor Schmidt first called attention to the problem of Soviet regional nuclear deployments in late 1977, the Carter Administration argued that NATO missile modernization was unnecessary because the U.S. defense pledge held firm. But once sold on the idea, Washington may have appeared to come on too vigorously in support of what was originally, and should have remained, an initiative of West European governments. It was soon made to appear that a domineering Pentagon was forcing cruise and Pershing II missiles upon a reluctant Europe, even though throughout the negotiation of the SALT II accords it had been the European allies who were most disturbed over the possible precedent-setting effect of the Protocol on their ability to acquire cruise missiles later. The image of an erratic and unpredictable Alliance leader was compounded when it became clear, even before the Soviet invasion of

Afghanistan, that the Senate would not give consent to the ratification of SALT II.

By 1980 there were a lot of sensible and responsible people in Western Europe who, while gratified that NATO had been able in December 1979 to achieve some appearance of unanimity on a delicate defense issue[2] (following the mishandled neutron warhead fiasco), nevertheless harbored misgivings over the future of U.S. and NATO nuclear strategies. Some NATO field commanders were expressing doubts about the utility of the shorter-range tactical nuclear weapons (e.g., the howitzers), fearing that they would be overrun before authorization to fire them was received. In the latter 1970s the Netherlands became officially committed to a shift of emphasis from nuclear to conventional defense, and to a reduction in the number of nuclear "tasks" performed by Dutch forces and the number of nuclear weapons stationed on Dutch territory.[3] Given the changes which had occurred in the strategic and Eurostrategic military environments, weapons which had once been looked upon as pillars of deterrence were now looked upon as invitations to disaster if war should break out.

There does exist, then, a political-strategic matrix in which concern among defense-knowledgeable elites about NATO's present posture of deterrence and defense is understandable. Most incumbent policymakers in NATO countries wish to solve the perceived problem by redressing the military imbalance in Europe and establishing greater "symmetry of vulnerability" between Western Europe and the Soviet Union through the "two-track" approach of INF deployment and negotiations over permitted INF levels. It is possible that some policymakers in NATO governments, who formally supported the need for the Alliance's nuclear modernization, may have quietly welcomed the peace movement as a political excuse for postponement of missile deployment as long as possible while demonstrating maximum flexibility in the arms talks at Geneva. In view of the fragility and thin parliamentary margins of governing parties and coalitions in various West European countries in recent years, much of the subtle maneuvering that went on from 1979 to 1981 can be explained in terms of linkage between external diplomacy and internal politics. (Since late 1981, electoral outcomes have produced more stable governments in Belgium, West Germany, Britain, and Italy.)

---

[2] The decision to install 572 Pershing II and cruise missiles in several European NATO countries, starting in 1983.

[3] R.D.M. Furlong, "Dutch Defense Policy for the '80s: Less Nuclear, More Conventional," *International Defense Review*, Vol. 12, No. 3 (1979), pp. 319-322; *Defence Budget 1980 Policy Report*, Ministry of Defence, The Hague, The Netherlands, n.d., pp. 9-15.

The Nature of the "Peace Movement"

The "peace movement" which has necessitated the maneuvering cannot be explained adequately by reference to practical political factors and the type of rational assessments and compromises which normally undergird Western democratic, parliamentary systems. The "peace movement" is an ingathering and an outpouring of feelings, emotions, enthusiasm, zeal, passion, righteousness, and the spirit of which crusading missions are made. It may be naively utopian in its professed goals and not very successful in offering solutions to problems, but it is quite shrewd in its methods of mobilizing protest and channeling resentment. Moreover, it is far from superficial in its underlying philosophical and religious *weltanschauung*. The advocates of peace and socio-economic justice through the radical transformation of existing institutional structures have often managed to preempt the high moral ground of idealism and spiritual principle from the advocates of freedom and human rights and those who would defend Western civilization, regardless of its deficiencies, against the totalitarian threat at its gates.

A few caveats are in order at this point. First, although the subject of this paper is the "peace movement in Western Europe," I surely do not wish to imply that those who demonstrate their protest against nuclear weapons hold any monopoly either of moral virtue or dedication to peace. No one wants nuclear war. The principal issue of our time pertains to choosing the policy course best calculated to prevent the outbreak of war. Here I strongly agree with Andrei Sakharov's conviction that eliminating the danger of nuclear war by restoring balance in the strategic and Eurostrategic dimensions demands a higher priority for the next decade than nuclear disarmament, and that it will probably be necessary to deploy both the intercontinental MX missile as well as intermediate-range forces (INF) in NATO for the purpose of reducing the risk-taking propensity of Soviet leaders.[4] In other words, the term "peace movement" is a misnomer. Political pacifism has never been known to head off a war. Ill conceived, it can contribute toward the onset of a war, as it did in the 1930s.

Furthermore, it is misleading to speak of a "movement" as if we were dealing with a homogeneous, monolithic phenomenon. The protest of recent years exhibits some common elements throughout Western Europe—for example, in the emotional slogans, propaganda and demonstration tactics employed against the acquisition of cruise and Pershing II missiles. But the "movement" varies considerably from Britain to Germany to France to the Netherlands to Italy. Within each country, it is made up of disparate elements—cadres and followers, political parties or factions thereof, women's

---

[4] Andrei Sakharov, "The Danger of Thermonuclear War: An Open Letter to Dr. Sidney Drell," *Foreign Affairs*, Summer 1983, pp. 1001-1016.

4

organizations, ecological groups, pacifist societies, squatters, social dropouts, and all sorts of *ad hoc* associations and individuals who participate alone to give their lives meaning or to escape from boredom. The protesters have received from the mass media an amount of attention quite disproportionate to their total numbers in the general population. Their ability to have a significant effect on the outcome of parliamentary elections, the formation of governing coalitions, and the taking of policy decisions has been exaggerated by the press and diminished by the actual choices of several national electorates in recent years. When the "movement" fails to move progressively from one success to another, some of its components begin to argue with each other over fundamental principles and blame each other's tactical approaches for the disastrous failures of the cause. This alone should be sufficient to demonstrate that there is no single, unified "movement."

Thus, the "peace movement" is neither coterminous with the West's aspirations and political efforts for peace nor a coherent political movement, except in the minds of mass media pundits and other *afficionados*. But since we have been saddled with the term as a shorthand expression for a contemporary "happening" in political sociology, we may be obliged to employ it occasionally—and appropriately—in quotation marks.

Philosophical Roots of the "Peace Movement"

There are some who would say that there is no necessity to spell out a philosophy or theology of the "peace movement," which they see as a purely contemporary political or sociological phenomenon not invested with any profound intellectual content. To be sure, the current antinuclear protest can be studied merely as another modern mass movement, subject to the usual laws of leadership, organization, propaganda, crowd psychology, and media-induced faddism. But a movement such as this one has to be able in its propaganda appeals to address ideas and values which large numbers of people regard as important. The cadres of the antinuclear campaign have achieved their success, at least in part, by playing on some themes which are deeply rooted in the thinking of educated Europeans.

A century and a third has passed since Karl Marx launched his critique of capitalism (including elements of praise for its accomplishments before damning it for its injustice). Two-thirds of a century has passed since Lenin began to equate peace with socialism and identified "capitalist imperialism" as the principal cause of international conflict and war. Western intellectuals have always been powerfully attracted to Marx's sociological analysis, dialectical materialism, economic determinism, and concept of the class struggle as the key to social and technological history, despite the recurring necessity for revisionist interpretations to adjust for the dismal failures of

5

Marx's predictions. Ever since 1917 the world has witnessed an intensive campaign to equate the "capitalist West" with ruthless exploitation of the poorer regions of the world and with preparations for war. This campaign has grown steadily more organized, more sophisticated, more scientific, and more effective, until it has affected the thinking of millions of the *lumpenintelligentsia* who would deny any sympathy for the basic tenets of Marxism-Leninism. So successful has the international propaganda effort been—based as it is on an essentially Pavlovian conditioning process—that large segments of the capitalist bourgeoisie and even larger segments of Western upper middle classes are often found to explain world events in Marxist-Leninist terms and to grow more and more suspicious of their own governments. It is now almost an article of faith: one must give Moscow the benefit of the doubt and mistrust Western parliamentary governments.

This is by no means to suggest that the Western "peace movement" is primarily a Soviet export. In one Western country after another, the effort to discredit pacifist, antinuclear and unilateral disarmament movements by portraying them as funded, advised, supported, manipulated, or directed by the Soviet Union and its well-known apparatus for infiltration, subversion, and agitation, including the World Peace Council, have failed to arouse any significant public reaction, especially among opinion leaders, regardless of the plausibility of evidence adduced in specific instances. The most that Western intellectuals are willing to admit is that the Soviet Union seeks to exploit the "peace movement" and turn it to its own political advantage, as is to be expected. Pavlovian conditioning and *le trahison des clercs* aside, Western intellectuals and media pundits will not readily abandon their role as Cardinal-Protectors of the "peace movement." That movement strikes some resonant emotional chords deep within the Western psyche. By sounding some very old and not-so-old themes out of Western philosophical and religious history, both the authentic indigenous prophets and cynical external puppeteers of the "peace movement" have been able to appeal powerfully to the sentiments of idealists throughout the West and to influential groups within society—youth, artists, writers, social critics of all sorts, scientists, teachers at all educational levels, the women's liberation movement, ecologists, television and radio commentators, newspaper columnists, and the religious establishment including priests, nuns, bishops, and the lay staff members of the ecclesiastical bureaucracy.

The ideologically committed zealots of the "peace movement" in Western Europe and, *mutatis mutandis*, their somewhat "pale reflection" counterparts in the U.S. nuclear freeze movement and associated pacifist organizations ("pale" because they are utterly innocent of any real philosophy) have sought to transform the single issue of new nuclear weapons programs—specifically, INF deployment in Europe and MX development in the United States—into a sort of litmus-paper test of the moral quality of Western civilization.

Political leaders of the NATO governments, who are responsible for the security of their societies and who are obliged to act out of political necessity rather than out of optimal personal moral choice, have found that it is usually not sufficient to counter a deeply rooted cultural phenomenon such as the current antinuclear movement with the kind of rational political-strategic arguments which are the stock-in-trade of professional analysts of international affairs. Although the "peace movement" has begun to acquire its own cadre of "counter-experts" who are familiar, in a hostile, contemptuous way, with the lexicon and thought modes of strategic analysts, hard-core ideological pacifists are not interested in engaging in serious debates over the subtler technical points of strategy—for this is the medium of discourse of a decadent, immoral culture. Anyone who suggests a calm debate is likely to be branded either an enemy or a hypocrite.

It is appropriate to take up philosophical developments first, for they preceded—by from one to three centuries—fundamental changes in Christian theology which led to the emergence of the Social Gospel, initially among Protestants and much more recently within the Catholic Church. One cannot write a complete recipe of the various philosophical ingredients that have gone into the contemporary "peace movement," which is a mixture of several different thought trends, psychological complexes and impulses, and social movements of resentment, reform, nihilism, anarchism, revolution, and utopian aspirations. Some of these elements are explicit; some of them perhaps only vaguely felt. Many of them are mutually contradictory—a fact which makes the "peace movement" a loose coalition often ideologically divided within itself, but held together by a common denominator of hatred for nuclear weapons—especially those possessed by the Western countries allied in NATO. In sum, the "peace movement"—as many commentators have noted—knows much better what it opposes than what it positively favors. But "anti" feeling is a powerful factor in politics. And nuclear weapons have come to be looked upon as the key symbol of the Western capitalist-industrial and "imperialist" culture, with all of its values, attitudes, and institutions that the "peace movement" despises. Herbert Marcuse and Jurgens Habermas see nuclear weapons as the ultimate absurd product of Western rationalism and democracy that bursts the bonds of loyalty of citizen to the liberal state which threatens him with extinction.

The Enlightenment. Despite the philosophical and ideological pluralism which imparts to the "peace movement" a certain "crazy quilt" aspect, it is possible to identify certain philosophical assumptions and themes of recent centuries which infuse it. Here primacy of place must go to those streams of thought which emanated from the Enlightenment. The Enlightenment, defined broadly to include such thinkers as Descartes, Spinoza,

7

Locke, Voltaire, Newton, Kant and others brought about a revolution in mathematics, empirical and theoretical science, and philosophy, thereby ushering in an Age of Reason to succeed the medieval age of Christian Faith. The same rational techniques which were pushing back the frontiers of scientific knowledge were expected to yield equally remarkable benefits when applied to all other dimensions of life—religion, politics, law, education, and economics. The misery and evil in the world would no longer be explained away resignedly by reference to Original Sin. The real obstacles to human progress were mystery, superstition, all forms of traditional authority, and the abyss of ignorance in which people were deliberately imprisoned by their oppressors. The function of reason was to criticize, ridicule, and tear down all obstacles to human emancipation—in short to be iconoclastic, not to justify the existing social order or venerate it as something sacred, handed down from the past and embodying the accumulated wisdom of many generations in its customary laws and traditional institutions and beliefs, as Aristotle and the medieval Scholastics had taught.

There is plenty of this spirit in the contemporary "peace movement" on both sides of the ocean. Antinuclear pacifist ideologues roundly condemn the rationalism of Western societies, yet exhibit a blind faith in their own reason. Children of the Enlightenment and its ensuing French Revolutionary ideals of *liberté, egalité,* and *fraternité,* they believe deeply in their own brands of democracy, science, and education as able to effect the salvation of the human race in the present crisis. They have nothing but contempt for the knowledge of nuclear strategists, political scientists, and experienced policymakers who are compelled in their positions of responsibility to try to understand and deal with the realities of international power. Throughout history ideologues have been quite adept at applying a form of critical, cynical, even witty Voltairean reason against the existing order—a kind of sophomoric logic which attacks by reducing things to simplicity and the apparent absurdity of contradiction, but which is disembodied from the political world as it really is rather than as philosophers might wish it to be. (Einstein once said: "We should try to make things as simple as possible, but not any simpler.")

A certain unrelenting mode of logic, says Chesterton, can often produce madness. Like Chesterton's madman, the minds of pacifist ideologues—when they cut themselves off from society and communicate almost exclusively with each other—think in logically consistent but constricted circles. They are capable of explaining to their own satisfaction a large number of things, but only in a small way, according to a single narrow standard. Lacking good, comprehensive, and balanced judgment, they perceive a sinister causality everywhere. Like Freud on sex, they are preoccupied with a single factor. They are so eminently logical on that one subject that it is futile to argue with them about it. We devise arguments to persuade ourselves more than them. What they require is not arguments but air.[5]

The *philosophes* of the Enlightenment also bequeathed to the modern Western world a fundamental optimism about human nature. Once we throw off the dead hand of the past, they believed with a touching faith, we shall find that human beings are intrinsically good and reasonable, filled with sympathy and compassion for each other. Evil has been institutionalized in the social structure because of ignorance, superstition, and oppressive authority, not because of any essential defect within us. Whereas Augustine had said that spiritually wounded human nature has inherited an in-eradicable *animus dominandi* or drive to power which must be recognized as fundamental in all political philosophies, Marx and all other modern utopians have believed that power relationships arise out of class structures or obsolete educational methods; once the proper transformations have been made, all prejudice, hatred, class consciousness, inequality, and exploitation will cease. A naive belief in the indefinite perfectibility and happiness of human beings, unmarred by any trace of tragedy, combined with the steady march of civilization into a warless future of justice and plenty, was a legacy of the Enlightenment which was taken even more seriously by Americans than by Europeans, but it still colors the thinking of many in the "peace movement." As Kenneth N. Waltz pointed out, modern utopians and the behavioral scientists who serve as their consultants and advisers on the causes and cures of social conflict seem to be saying in effect that if only human nature and behavior were completely different from what they are, we could easily solve the problems of security, armaments, and war by simply making them go away. Ardent pacifists fit into this category when they propose to bring about peace through the adoption of sudden, radical changes in the structure and policies of nations that simply are not feasible in the eyes of political scientists.[6]

Romanticism. Even more important than the Enlightenment legacy for understanding the peace movement is the Continental heritage of Romanticism, marked by strong anti-rationalist and anti-modernist biases. Rousseau was a Romantic more in love with nature and with natural and intuitive human impulses and emotions than with Descartes' clear, distinct, and abstract ideas. Subsequent European Romantics—especially the Germans (Schiller, Goethe, Beethoven, Heine, Fichte, Wagner and others)—were disenchanted in varying degrees with the excesses and perversions of Enlightenment rationalism. Like Luther before them, they despised the

---

[5] Gilbert K. Chesterton, *Orthodoxy* (New York: Dodd, Mead, 1949), pp. 31-34.
[6] Kenneth N. Waltz, *Man, the State and War* (New York: Columbia University Press, 1959), Chapter 3.

cold and callous intellectual abstractions of the philosophers. Watching the new tide of industrialism sweep across Europe from Britain, the Romantics lamented the passing of the traditional pre-industrial order. Even those who rejoiced in the liberation of the individual spirit wrought by the Revolution experienced a sense of loss at the atrophy of the human sentiments which went with community (*Gemeinschaft*)—consciousness of belonging to an order in which rights and duties were understood, where there was an organic unity of religion, culture, work, and social life, where custom and status were appropriately respected, where human beings knew friendship, affection, and sympathy. All this was giving way to what Ferdinand Tonnies would call *Gesellschaft*—a form of society held together by a web of cold, impersonal associations based on legal and monetary contracts.

The new society being born was marked by materialism and spiritual emptiness, as well as a driving determination to exploit and ravish a once-reverenced nature. The Romantics were deeply disturbed by the fact that mining and manufacturing operations were pillaging and blemishing nature. They sought escape from the sordid reality of industrialism, with its smoke and slums, not to mention the human misery described in Marx's deadening prose. Whereas Francis Bacon had hoped that science, by maintaining an ethical neutrality and avoiding questions of ultimate purpose and meaning, would be able to avert a conflict with organized religion, the Romantics did not try to conceal their aversion and contempt for "value-free" science. Sciences and humanities became two distinct cultures within the universities. Romantic humanists came to despise the world of mechanical precision and organizational efficiency—the whole scientific-technological-bureaucratic-commercial order of predictability and routinization, shorn of all mystery and spontaneity.

Enlightenment rationalism and Romantic anti-rationalism and anti-modernism have coexisted in dialectical tension for a long time in European culture, producing a collective cognitive dissonance and a gnawing psychological unease about the direction of social evolution, affecting large numbers of people in one degree or another—not only extremists or sensitive individuals of an intellectual or artistic bent, but even normal, moderate middle class elements that strive to preserve continuity amidst change, security amidst instability. Particularly in Germany, the tensions contributed to the exacerbation of tendencies already present in elements of the Teutonic tradition—*angst*, cultural pessimism, and an anti-liberal skepticism of parliamentary institutions. From Bismarck to the Weimar Republic, heirs of the Romantic tradition were unable to generate any enthusiasm for liberal parliamentarianism, which was associated with the bourgeois industrial order and with unedifying efforts to decide what was right and good for the nation not by consulting the *Volksgeist* (or in France, Rousseau's *volonté générale*) but by manipulating morally indifferent majority compromises among parties, factions, and organized interest groups more anxious to feather their own nests than to act on the basis of noble principles. In Germany and Italy, the middle and professional classes finally sought escape from the boredom and meaninglessness of liberal-industrial life by embracing Nazism and Fascism. By the 1930s, among the major Western powers liberal representative government was still held in esteem only in Britain and the United States, countries which were inviting fascist aggression with their public postures of pacifism, appeasement, and isolationism. It is easy to detect a revival of this Romantic anti-parliamentary streak in the Greens.

We need not trace in detail the Romantics' anti-industrial animus through the French utopian socialists (who favored substituting the "administering of things" for the "governing of men"—but in work-and-life enterprises on a small, voluntary scale); through the European and American anarchists (who opposed all instruments of statism and modern governmental coercion—police, courts, prisons, armies and bureaucracies of planners and inspectors—while favoring purely voluntary cooperative associations); through the episode of machinery-smashing by the Luddites in Britain; down to respectable modern conservationists and environmentalists campaigning against strip mining, the chemical pollution of air, forests, streams, rivers and oceans, and any product of the military-industrial state which threatens the biosphere not only for human beings but for any endangered species down to the lowly snail darter.

Marxism. The third important philosophical stream feeding the contemporary peace movement is Marxism and its principal offshoots—democratic socialism and Soviet communism. Marx added his powerful voice as scientific prophet to the Romantics' moral critique of bourgeois capitalism and its value system; he furnished an essentially utopian vision of a happy classless society as the culmination of the historic conflict of oppressors and oppressed; and he supplied a fetching explanation of why man is alienated from his own creative work, and how artist-worker and product will be rejoined after the negation of the negation. But Marx was not a Romantic by any stretch of the imagination. He had nothing but contempt for the Romantic elements in the thinking of such utopian socialists as Saint-Simon and Fourier or the anarchist Proudhon. Marxist socialist parties, while preaching human liberation, equality, and pacifism/disarmament in bourgeois capitalist societies, were nevertheless fundamentally at odds with all Romantic tendencies because Marxists are hyper-rationalists and even more materialistic and committed to economic-technological development than capitalists, not a bit less determined to amass capital through the mastery and exploitation of nature. (Today, the Marxist societies of Eastern Europe are much less concerned about environmental pollution than Western "capitalist" societies are.)

11

Furthermore, Marxists are much more thoroughly dedicated to strengthening the bureaucratic, planning state than are liberal capitalists, who only reluctantly accept the degree of regulation required for mixing publicly planned social welfare with the free market economy. Marxists molded in Leninist ways of thought (not the Revisionist followers of Kautsky and Bernstein) loathe parliamentarianism for their own reasons. It makes the workers become addicted to piecemeal reform and amelioration of the industrial system through the ballot box, whereas Marx looked for the increasing alienation and immiseration of workers until the climactic breaking point of revolution was inevitably reached. But the greatest failure of Marxism in the eyes of Romantics, anarchists and cultural pessimists consists in the fact that it aims at solving the problems of capitalism principally by changing the ownership pattern; it does not reverse the process of economic-technological growth; it does not deal with the main concern of Romantics—the dehumanizing effects of severing man from nature and transforming culture from the organic to the mechanistic. Although Western intellectuals carried on a love affair with Soviet communism through the early 1930s, the bloom wore off once the nature of Stalinism was fully revealed.

Despite occasional appearances of "loosening up," "liberalization," "peaceful coexistence," and "detente," which some Western analysts cite as evidence of "convergence" by two superpowers facing the essentially similar problems of "post-industrial society," the system which Lenin built has never been able to abandon its tyrannical oppression, only to subtilize its methods. Peace activists deny any wish to apologize for what goes on in Eastern Europe and the Soviet Union; sometimes they are even critical. (The Eurocommunist parties themselves profess a hatred of the Gulag syndrome.) Purist Romantics in the "peace movement," as we have seen, have serious ideological disagreements with all "developmental Marxists"— whether democratic socialists or communists. But the European "peace movement" in general shies away from anticommunism as an instrument of capitalist propaganda, designed to buttress a detested status quo in the West. The "peace movement" did little to protest the Soviet-backed suppression of Solidarity in Poland, contenting itself to lie low until the crisis subsided while taking credit for the fact that the existence of the "peace movement" actually protected Poland against a more ruthless and bloody crackdown by Soviet forces. Like Western leftist intellectuals in general, who have never quite managed to forget their infatuation with communism in the 1930s, the mythmakers of the "peace movement" continue to evaluate the Western democracies according to the standards of Jefferson and Wilson, and the communist countries by those of Lenin. Thus, they are willing to enter a tactical alliance with communism, which they distrust far less than capitalism. Indeed, they attribute some of the worst defects of the communist system to American capitalism, whose threats have forced the Soviet Union to emulate it. They fear Americanization more than Sovietization of Europe.

Existentialism. The fourth and last major philosophical input into the "peace movement" to be treated here is Existentialism, which represents a radical rejection of the Enlightenment concept of man as a rational being, capable of solving his problems and progressing toward perfection. Existentialists may be Christian or atheist. Both view man as an alienated being, destined for unrelieved *angst*, trouble, suffering, and tragedy on this earth. Such Christian thinkers as Dostoyevsky and Kirkegaard anathematized both the capitalist and socialist visions of society because they are based on the premise that man *does* live by bread alone, as well as the blasphemous thought that happiness can be achieved in this life without God. Human alienation, they believed, cannot be overcome except through the "I-Thou" relationship: personal recognition of sinfulness, personal repentance and dependence, divine redemption, and personal salvation beyond history. They had no doubt that Marxism and all other utopian blueprints for the establishment of a perfectly rational social order are bound to lead to demoniacal tyranny over the human spirit.

Atheist Existentialists from Nietzsche to Sartre derided modern society's quest for happiness as futile. The individual (who alone has reality, in contrast to the abstraction known as society) achieves authentic existence only by squarely confronting tentativeness, ambiguity, contradiction, alienation, spiritual anguish, and the reality of suffering and death. Christian and atheist Existentialists either foresaw or accepted with resignation the twin monsters they regarded as offspring of Enlightenment reason—the totalitarianism which extinguishes the human spirit and hyperbolic development of science and technology (reaching a climax in nuclear weapons) which now threatens humanity with physical extinction. The choice facing the individual—slavery or annihilation—contains an agonistic dilemma which is particularly exquisite for the Existentialist, for it symbolizes acutely the hopelessness of the human situation. Whether Christian or atheist, the Existentialist finds amusing, poignant, or sad the ever increasing number of misguided people who dash about madly, picturing themselves as saviors of mankind. For the atheist, there is no savior; for the Christian, salvation has already occurred once for all, but its fulfillment for the individual must be patiently awaited. (New Left Catholic liberation theologians, however, are determined to move the Kingdom of God from hereafter to here and now.)

Existentialist ideas, then, stand in negative critique of the "peace movement" insofar as ideological pacifists hope to escape from *angst* and lead mankind in the ascent from Plato's Cave. But paradoxically, Existentialist strands of thought have also served as positive supports of the "peace movement." They help to explain some of the nihilistic attitudes prevalent among

13

European youth today, including the spreading conviction that the values of Western civilization are not worth defending—certainly not at the potential cost of nuclear war. The Existentialist tenet that human beings are fundamentally irrational, buttressed by vestiges of Freudianism, memories of fascism, and abundant historical experience of individual and collective psychological aberrations, lends theoretical respectability to the insistence of the peace movement that the rational decision-making processes on which strategists base the effectiveness of nuclear deterrence is bound to break down under the psychological strains of a future crisis. This type of thinking, perhaps more than any other, lends itself to the "bumper-stickerization" of philosophy and the vulgarization of strategic thought: "We have never developed weapons that we have not used." "We must end the arms race before the arms race ends us." "We have enough to kill everybody several times over." "The way to stop is to stop. Support the nuclear freeze." "Nuclear war will be started not by madmen but by leaders who could pass every sanity test devised by the capitalist system."

Existentialism also breeds its own love of living dangerously as a means of toning up an otherwise dull existence. It might make a small number of peace activists willing to assume considerable personal risk to advance the cause by carrying out acts of resistance or terror. But for the mainstream devotees of the movement, this tendency will probably be outweighed by the assignment of a high philosophical priority to biological survival as the ultimate goal of the species.

The probability that only a few antinuclearists may have been sufficiently steeped in Existentialism to be willing to offer their lives for the cause never meant that NATO governments expected to deploy the new missiles without opposition. For nearly two years, organizers had been talking about and planning a shift from protest demonstrations to "direct action" against INF installation. London and Bonn were ready for the civil disobedience which materialized at Greenham Common and Mütlangen in late 1983. The movement was divided between a large majority—probably more than four-fifths of its actives—who favored only nonviolent resistance and a small minority who were willing, at least in theory, to condone violence even if many of them were not ready to practice it themselves. It takes only a small number of "nihilists," of course, to wreak havoc through violent action. The overwhelming majority of all West Europeans, however, abhor violence. Those who have no moral scruples over resorting to the methods of terroristic anarchism—and most anarchists are not terrorists—are likely, therefore, to refrain from extreme deeds which would prove counterproductive and badly damage the cause. Thus, while some may have been tempted to engage in sabotage, most eschewed tactics that went beyond nonviolent resistance and obstruction—sit-ins, "chain-ins" and "die-ins" (emulating death by radioactivity), blockading military movement, and trying to provoke

14

repressive or violent response from NATO government military or police forces.

The Politics of Protest

The foregoing sketchy references to the complex and sometimes contradictory elements in modern European philosophical thought may help to improve our understanding of the "peace movement" as a bundle of profound resentments against the materialism and consumerism of modern Western "capitalist" society—even though Marx could no longer recognize it as capitalist; against the accent on the acquisition of money and power (even though the peace movement wants more of both, but for its own holy cause); against industrialism, technology, and the ravishing of the natural environment (as if the world's expanding population will be able to make do with ever fewer resources in the future—candlepower and horsepower, presumably, if only we had enough bees and horses—without reaching the point of global, self-inflicted economic holocaust); against bigness in all forms—big machines, big corporations, big governmental bureaucracies which callously disregard the needs of the excluded ones (the poor, the hungry, the squatters, the social drop-outs, the drug addicts, the gays); and above all against the military balance, military alliances, the division of Europe, the presence of nuclear weapons, and the specter of nuclear war. From the foregoing analysis it is fairly easy to see that the absorption of the ecological (especially the antinuclear power) movement by the "peace movement" in an "eco-peace" coalition was inevitable. What is harder to understand is the fact that the European "peace movement" vents its spleen more against NATO than the Warsaw Pact, more against Washington than Moscow, and more against the nuclear weapons which defend Western Europe than those which target it—except perhaps that, being more alienated from the American culture it knows than the Soviet culture it does not know, it is more bent on avoiding new U.S. missile deployments than reducing older and recent Soviet ones.

The "peace movement" has also become infused with a neonationalism of the left in Germany, where—increasingly under the tutelage of the antinuclear, anti-system Green Party—it is raising questions concerning the viability of parliamentary institutions, the value of party politics in Germany, the possibility of a new social order in the Federal Republic, the division of Germany, and the presence of foreign troops on the soil of the two German states. Thus, the "peace movement" is contributing to a revival of the issue of the political reunification of the *Kulturnation* as a challenge both to the present socio-economic structure and the diplomatic-military status quo in Central Europe. West German pacifism in the postwar period has always been ostensibly in favor of "neutralism" and demilitarization,

15

but pro-Soviet in its opposition to West German integration into NATO and the European Community, and in its conviction that the question of German unity can be settled only on the basis of friendly relations with, and on terms acceptable to, the Soviet Union. The antinuclear and neutralist movements lost their firm institutional base when the SPD grudgingly accepted the Adenauer state in the 1959 Godesberg Program; the movements languished through the era of *Ostpolitik*, but they have been galvanized into new life in the last three years. The rise of the Greens may motivate the SPD to move to the left rather than be outflanked, to rekindle its traditional pacifism, and to pursue policies aimed at allowing a more neutral FRG to put distance between itself and the United States.[7]

The Role of the Christian Churches

The antinuclear protest movement has been substantially strengthened in recent years by the addition of large numbers of members of the Christian Churches. Only in the Netherlands did a religious organization take the lead in arousing popular sentiment over the issue of nuclear weapons. That was in 1977-1978, when the Inter-Church Peace Council (IKV) gathered a million or so signatures on petitions objecting to the deployment by the United States of enhanced radiation warheads (misnamed "neutron bombs") in NATO. With that development, the moribund anti-Vietnam War "peace movement" in Western Europe was resuscitated to a new life. Since then, in West Germany, Britain and elsewhere, the Churches have become more actively involved in the public debate over nuclear strategies and weapons, thereby lending social respectability to the antinuclear campaign. If the movement's cadres have come largely from professional lifetime pacifists and antimilitarists, haters of capitalism, industrialism, consumerism and Americanization, ecologists and advocates of women's liberation, communists, left-wing democratic socialists, anti-modernist Romantics, cultural pessimists, anti-parliamentarians, pro-neutral nationalists, disgruntled intellectuals, former hippies, and social dropouts of every variety, it must be said that the rank-and-file numbers which have given the movement genuine political clout have come from the respectable and middle class members of Protestant and Catholic Churches.

Antinuclear protest campaigns waxed and waned in Britain and Germany for two decades for the simple reason that they lacked a solid sociological base among workers and their political parties during the period of economic recovery, growth and integration. Not until the economic slowdown

---

[7] Kim R. Holmes, "The West German Peace Movement and the National Question: German Identity, Alternative Culture and the Politics of Peace," Unpublished manuscript, April 1983, pp. 10-25.

16

induced by the energy crisis did the labor parties of Western Europe begin to flag in their staunch support of NATO and U.S. deterrence policy, especially in Britain and the Netherlands, and in the left wing of the SPD. The "peace movement" felt a surge of hope that the old antinuclearism and pacifism of democratic socialism could be rekindled. Just at that time the Dutch IKV brought hundreds of thousands of Church members, mostly Protestant, into the great struggle to fulfill the goal: "Nuclear weapons out of the world, and first out of the Netherlands." From that time on, it was a new sociological phenomenon with a new moralistic slogan: "Make peace without weapons."

It is by now well established that pacifism as the unconditional and conscientious renunciation of war by the individual appeared in history only with the rise of Christianity. Although there are no New Testament texts explicitly condemning warfare or the soldier's profession, Christian pacifists have always based their position on what they interpreted the spirit of the Christ of the Gospels to require. The first three centuries of Church history show a strong intellectual sentiment in favor of pacifism and against Christians serving in the military, but we must remember that what we have from the patristic period are the writings of well-educated intellectuals who in almost every age manifest an anti-military bias. Besides doctrinal pacifism, there were several other compelling reasons why Christians would not wish to volunteer for service in the Roman army—the temptations of camp life, the obligation to perform idolatrous practices, the use of the army to persecute Christians, etc. In any event, the Church did not officially forbid military service for Christians. Knowing Old Testament history, the orthodox Church Fathers could not possibly hold the waging of war to be intrinsically evil.[8]

According to the traditional doctrine of the just war, which represented a fusion of ancient Graeco-Roman thought and practical Christian wisdom, Christ's life and death in the Gospels was not regarded as an appropriate model for the action of political communities. The individual Christian seeking perfection should turn the other cheek instead of asserting a claim to personal justice. But the state, since it is responsible for safeguarding a common good, which has meaning only here and now, cannot turn the other cheek. It must use force when necessary to uphold the order of justice and

---

[8] From the voluminous literature available, only a few samples need be mentioned: Peter Brock, *Pacifism in Europe to 1914* (Princeton, N.J.: Princeton University Press, 1972), Chapter 1; Roland H. Bainton, *Christian Attitudes Toward War and Peace* (Nashville, Tenn.: Abingdon Press, 1960), Chapters 4 and 5; Edward A. Ryan, S.J., "The Rejection of Military Service by the Early Christian," *Theological Studies*, March 1952; Knut Willem Ruyter, "Pacifism and Military Service in the Early Church," *Cross Currents*, Spring 1982.

protect its people. The Christian may voluntarily choose martyrdom, but no one has the right to try to impose martyrdom on the whole community.[9]

We need not examine the traditional criteria for the right to go to war (*ius ad bellum*) and for the rightful conduct of the war (*ius in bello*), except to say that the two most important principles for the nuclear age are (1) proportionality—the cause must be of sufficient gravity to warrant the widespread death and destruction which modern war entails; and (2) discrimination—the killing of innocent noncombatants may not be directly intended, even though a large number of indirect, unintended casualties (in keeping with the criterion on proportionality) may be unavoidable. Just war, then, must be limited war. But the compromise that has to be made between morality, humanitarianism, and civilization on the one hand and military necessity on the other has always been extremely difficult to evaluate, and moralists have always had to be vague on the subject.[10]

As war became more total in theory and practice in the late nineteenth and early twentieth centuries, Christian ethicians became increasingly uncomfortable at the thought that the old principles were breaking down and that modern military technology was making it almost impossible for the conditions of the just war to be fulfilled. Nevertheless, there were very few Catholic or orthodox Protestant conscientious objectors during World War II, despite the fact that it took tens of millions of lives. However, the obliteration and atomic bombing of cities was subsequently condemned. In 1954, Pope Pius XII warned that when war escapes from the control of man and annihilates life over wide areas it must be rejected as immoral, but he did not condemn nuclear weapons as evil in themselves, nor did he label every use of them under all circumstances illicit.

The debate over nuclear weapons has gone on longer and more intensively among some Protestant bodies than within the Catholic Church, but for many years that debate did not produce a significant political impact because of the greater divergence of Protestant opinion and the weaker moral authority of the Churches deriving from their diffuse structure.[11] While Protestants and British Catholics were moving toward "nuclear pacifism" before 1960, Pius XII strongly reaffirmed the doctrine of the just war at the time of Hungary in 1956, and two eminent American theologians—Protestant

---

[9] See Bainton, *op. cit.*, Chapter 6; G.I.A.D. Draper, "The Origins of the Just War Tradition," *New Blackfriars*, November 1964; Joan D. Tooke, *The Just War in Aquinas and Grotius* (London: SPCK, 1965); James R. Childress, "Just-War Theories," *Theological Studies*, September 1978.

[10] Paul Ramsey, *The Just War: Force and Political Responsibility* (New York: Charles Scribner's Sons, 1968); James Turner Johnson, *Just War Tradition and the Restraint of War: A Moral and Historical Inquiry* (Princeton, N.J.: Princeton University Press, 1981); William V. O'Brien, *The Conduct of Just and Limited War* (New York: Praeger, 1981).

[11] L. Bruce van Voorst, "The Churches and Nuclear Deterrence," *Foreign Affairs*, Spring 1983, pp. 838-840.

Paul Ramsey and Catholic Jesuit John Courtney Murray—decried the rise of "sentimental pacifism" and envisaged the possibility that the discriminating use of nuclear weapons against unjust aggression might someday be necessary and morally permissible.

The Protestants had led the way to the Social Gospel at least a half century before the Catholics began to move in that direction with the Second Vatican Council. One of the many changes brought about by that Council in 1965 was to support legal provisions for conscientious objection, just as the United States and the American Catholic Church were about to become deeply divided over the Vietnam War. Within a few years, the American Catholic bishops, who had previously been superpatriotic in their support for U.S. wars, followed Protestant and Jewish bodies in calling for selective conscientious objection as a corollary of the just war doctrine (not of pacifism) and as a moral right of conscience, but the U.S. Congress refused to grant citizens the legal right to pick and choose the wars in which they would be willing to fight.

The Vietnam War helped to radicalize a substantial segment of the American Catholic Church, among youth, academics, and the younger clergy. It is worth noting that four-fifths of all presently active bishops in the United States were consecrated after January 1, 1968, and all of the bishops' formal pronouncements on conscientious objection, war, peace, and nuclear weapons came after that "watershed year." The younger generation of "Jadot bishops" (named for the Apostolic Delegate in Washington who played a major role in their selection) were chosen for their pastoral experience, not as previously for their training in Rome and their knowledge of how the ecclesiastical bureaucracy works.[12]

Since Vatican II, younger Catholic theologians have pressed for alterations in belief-idea formulas that go considerably beyond what the Council Fathers approved in their restatement of traditional doctrine in contemporary idiom. The most significant new developments are political theology in Germany and liberation theology in Latin America, both of which have influenced the thinking of the younger generation of American Catholic theologians and clergy. Political theology, associated with Johannes Metz and the Protestant (Calvinist) Jurgen Moltmann, insists that all reality must be measured in the light of the promised Kingdom of God, which is not a state of blessedness in heaven beyond time but a model to be approached in the here and now. What we have here is a new "hermeneutic" or interpretation of the faith based on Scriptures which demands that Christianity undergo a deprivatization and a socialization, a shift of theological emphasis

---

[12] Marjorie Hyer, "How Our War-Blessing Catholic Bishops Got Religion on Nukes," *The Washington Post*, May 1, 1983.

from individual sin, repentance, and salvation to social sin, collective repentance, and the radical transformation of socio-economic structures. The bishops' synod in Rome in 1971 declared that the achievement of justice is constitutive of the Church's evangelical mission in the world. This means that it is the task of the Church not only to teach all nations but to change the world. The meaning of Christian hope is thereby altered; it becomes the virtue by which Christians assume responsibility for the shape of the future—not only their personal futures but the future of the whole world. The response of the European political theologians to the "God is dead" announcement is to prove the validity of Christianity by setting out to build a more human world of justice and peace.[13]

The Latin American liberation theologians present both a special case and critique of European political theology. They deny the "God is dead" premise, even though they concede that this may be appropriate as a starting point for secular, materialist Europe. But as they see it, God and the Church are alive and well in Latin America. The problem arises not from the decline of Church relevance to industrially advanced societies, as in Europe and the United States, but from the fact that the Church, which is of crucial importance in Latin American societies, has historically been on the wrong side. The Church must be brought over to the cause of revolution on behalf of the oppressed classes. Such theologians as Juan Luis Segundo, Leonardo Boff, and Gustavo Gutierrez preach that Jesus must no longer be looked upon as *Salvador* but as *Liberatador.*[14] Social justice in this world becomes a more urgent goal than that longed-for happiness in the next which Marx derided as "the sigh of the oppressed." Ever since the 1968 Latin American bishops' conference at Medellin, Colombia, the Church has emphasized support for the poor and the oppressed, and its own role as an agent of social justice. During the last two decades, many Catholic and Protestant theorists have transmuted the just war doctrine into a doctrine of justified revolutionary violence in "wars of national liberation" against "oppressive capitalist-imperialist systems" whose very institutions are redefined as the "new violence."

The Christian New Left has become highly selective from a political standpoint. It propounds a curious dialectical mixture of pacifism and opposition to the defense programs of the United States and the NATO Alliance on one hand, with active support on the other hand for violent anti-Western insurgency movements in Africa and Latin America. Furthermore, the New Christian Left, both Catholic and Protestant, sees the campaign against nuclear weapons as the most popular in a long list of "liberal" causes which

---

[13] Richard P. McBrien, *Catholicism* (Oak Grove, Minn.: Winston Press, 1981), pp. 60, 318, 697-701.
[14] *Ibid.*, pp. 491-492 and 698-699, and Francis P. Fiorenza, "Political Theology and Liberation Theology," in Thomas M. McFadden, editor, *Liberation, Revolution and Freedom* (New York: Seabury, 1975).

20

it has been militantly espousing for many years—the rights of women, homosexuals, and divorced and remarried persons within the Church, the rights of priests to marry and laicized priests to teach Catholic theology, the democratization of Church structures, the withdrawal of Church investments from a variety of multinational corporations and other "capitalist-imperialist oppressive" enterprises, and so forth. Nuclear pacifism is now expected by some to validate and lend respectability to all the other counter-cultural tendencies within the Churches.

Paul VI tried to hold a turbulent post-Vatican-II Church together by combining a progressive approach to socio-economic matters with a theological conservatism. He therefore favored a moderate nonviolent liberation theology in Latin America while avoiding any appearance of preaching liberation in Eastern Europe. Pope John Paul II has sought to redress what he sees as an imbalance by supporting human rights in Eastern Europe while trying to tone down the liberation theologians in Latin America by reminding them that the function of the Church is to teach and give witness, but not to become an active agent in the political order, since temporal matters lie properly within the sphere of competence of the laity. For this he is often called reactionary by the New Left, and excessively preoccupied with the Polish problem.

Some American Catholics of the Left undoubtedly see the nuclear weapons issue as a means of driving a wedge between Rome and the U.S. bishops, who in their recent pastoral letter on war and peace have gone beyond the Popes of the nuclear age and Vatican II in their attitude toward nuclear deterrence. Whereas Pope John Paul II, in his message to the U.N. General Assembly's Second Special Session on Disarmament in June 1982 called nuclear deterrence "morally acceptable" under prevailing circumstances, the American bishops have hedged deterrence with so many limitations, reservations, and caveats as to erode its credibility by coming close to denying the moral right of the U.S. government to do any effective planning for nuclear hostilities or to maintain a public operational strategic doctrine that would have sufficient plausibility to deter the broad spectrum of threats which are posed by Soviet nuclear and conventional capabilities. The World Council of Churches, at its Vancouver Assembly in August 1983, went beyond the Catholics by calling nuclear deterrence morally unacceptable and the possession of nuclear weapons, even for deterrence, "a crime against humanity."

Perhaps the most controversial policy recommendation in the bishops' pastoral letter is the call for NATO to enhance its conventional deterrent capabilities to the point of being able to renounce the option of first use of nuclear weapons. For more than two decades, U.S. administrations have been trying to persuade the European allies to strengthen conventional forces, but Europeans prefer to rely upon nuclear deterrence, provided that it is credible, rather than upon a conventional defense that would certainly be much more costly and probably less effective in preventing war. In actuality, NATO has never been able to back away too far from a nuclear strategy.

Another significant feature of the pastoral letter, one that has received almost no attention thus far in the media, is the strong emphasis which it places upon the need for developing "programmed methods" of non-violent resistance. If taken seriously and acted upon by large numbers of Catholics at some future time when conscription might have to be resumed, this would signal to the other side that Catholics are not only unwilling to condone the first use of nuclear weapons under any circumstances, but that they are also unwilling to bear arms even in a just conventional war of defense against aggression. Some European Catholics undoubtedly fear that they may be the first victims of the growing nuclear and general pacifism of their coreligionists across the ocean.

Conclusion

All can sympathize with the bishops and the antinuclear protesters when they utter their anguished, resounding "No" to nuclear war. Wishing and saying "No," however, are not enough. The decisions for war and peace are not taken by churches, political parties, peace societies, women's organizations, environmental groups, or hundreds of thousands of demonstrators. Those decisions are always taken by governments. What is required today is intelligent political leadership, indeed, statesmanship, in the East and the West. This alone can produce, through a reasonable combination of weapons modernization programs and arms negotiations, a stable political-military equilibrium, a form of mutual deterrence in which neither side feels itself at an unfair disadvantage or subject to undue intimidation. Unless both sides can achieve a symmetrical sense of legitimate security, there can be no climate favorable to a genuine improvement in East-West relations.

Clear, calm, rational thought is of the utmost importance at the present time. A highly emotional, ideological approach which arouses widespread hysterical fears that deterrence is certain to fail and that nuclear war is about to break out at any moment is not at all conducive to constructive diplomacy. A frantic antinuclearism of the type which is now coursing through the West—but not in the East, unfortunately—can itself help to undermine deterrence by tempting the adversary to undertake imprudent risks and press his luck too far. In this connection, it is encouraging to note that the French and German bishops, who are much closer to the zone of first encounter, and who are more familiar with the twin dangers of war and totalitarian tyranny, have exhibited a delicate and balanced appreciation of the political-psychological subtleties of nuclear deterrence, for which they have had some kind words.

As we know, the late autumn of 1983 in Western Europe, when preparations were being completed for the deployment of 16 Tomahawk cruise missiles in Britain and 9 Pershing-II missiles in West Germany,[15] was not nearly as "hot" as the media had predicted. The demonstrations at Greenham Common and at Mütlangen were not unmanageable. The tapering off of ardor and the decline in the magnitude of the antinuclear protest movement were due no doubt to several factors: the downing of the Korean airliner in late August, smoldering public resentment against Soviet suppressive policies in Afghanistan and Poland, and the determination of the NATO governments to proceed with long-planned efforts to redress the growing Eurostrategic nuclear balance if no substantial progress could be achieved in the arms control talks at Geneva. NATO simply could not bestow upon Moscow the monopoly right to carry out nuclear modernization while vetoing the reciprocal right of the Western Alliance.

The final Soviet ploy—walking out of the INF negotiations—proved to be a rather futile gesture. Far from fanning the flames of antinuclear protest in the West, it helped to damp them further. It also created a new international environment for codifying a genuine strategic equilibrium and renewing talks in the future with an improved chance of reaching viable, equitable agreements. The peace movement has left its mark, heavily in the West, lightly in the East. Whether it can ultimately produce symmetrical effects upon thinking in West and East remains to be seen.

---

[15] In March 1984, 16 Tomahawk cruise missiles were also installed at Comiso, Sicily, after a delay for technical reasons related to site preparations.

Democratic Ideals and the Problems of War and Peace in the Nuclear Age

by Midge Decter

D EMOCRACY, IDEALS, war, peace—these are all immensely large words. Far too large, taken in the abstract, to treat adequately in a short essay. Indeed, tomes have been written—and by the world's greatest thinkers— on each of these freighted terms. My more modest and pragmatic task will be to assess the current state of democratic values and institutions as we confront the moral dilemmas of nuclear warfare and the very real threat of Soviet expansionism.

When we, here and now, speak of war and peace, for example, what we are actually talking about is the perilous state of relations between East and West. Indeed, even the terms "East" and "West" are too vague and general: essentially they refer to the United States, Western Europe, and Japan on the one side and the Soviet bloc on the other.

The term "democratic," on the other hand, is too precise. When we use it, we almost always mean something broader and more elusive than gover- nance through the will of the majority: as we know, majority rule, un- moderated and unhampered, is tyranny. No, what we mean by "democratic" is no more than a rough, shorthand designation of that group of nations, most of them descending from Christendom, whose political institutions have for a little over two centuries successfully extended to ever greater numbers of their citizens the liberties of free men. We mean, in other words, that collection of institutions and traditions, attitudes and values, that goes by the name of Western Civilization. If these definitions are neither elegant nor altogether satisfactory, at least we all understand them, by our com- mon experience—both good and bad—in the same way.

Idealism and the Peace Movement

As for ideals, I believe the time has come when we should not speak of them at all. For those of us who have managed to survive intact into the 1980s, ideals are debased things. Too many crimes have been committed in their name. Too many criminals have been absolved from ordinary human responsibility on the ground that they have been guided by some imputed higher aspiration.

For nearly two decades now we have watched the privileged youth of our respective countries set out to destroy themselves, and the rest of us along with them, all the while seeking, and to our shame finding, justification

24

in something they and we have seen fit to call "ideals." What awaited these young people in the adult world, honeyed over though it was with wealth, ease, and the full range of private choices, was nevertheless only an imperfect mortal existence. Life promised them difficulties and obligations and moral necessities. So they simply refused that world—and the life it offered—with evasion, narcissism, drugs, suicide, and infantile (in this case literally infantile) leftism. And they spoke always, and were commonly spoken of by their elders, in language that harkened to their ideals.

In some important sense, the young were right to speak of themselves in this way. They *were* being idealistic. Not in the honorific sense of putting principle above love of self but in the sense of rejecting that which was in actuality there before them—in rejecting, in other words, ordinary life. There may be no greater truth for our time than that contained in the old adage: The perfect is the enemy of the good. The perfect has also long provided a handy antidote to the need to make serious moral choices, as in the question, "Since Western society is wanting in this or that respect, why should we differentiate it from the society of the Soviet Union?" To be idealistic, utopian, then, is to do away with the need to be moral.

The "peace movement" of today, in Europe and the United States, is the true spiritual legacy of those much touted and self-deceived young people of the 1960s and 1970s. The "peace movement" does not love peace; it hates the world.

Politicians who wish to display their bona fides as feeling, sensitive souls never refer to the peace movement without pointing out that it is made up of decent people. Particularly when such politicians are engaged in tracing the influence of the Soviet Union on this movement do they seem impelled to express their conviction that most of its members, though perhaps misguided, are moved by the highest motives. The truth is, *they are not decent people.* They may not be Soviet agents, but they are in a certain sense something worse. They are idealists, which is to say, moral evaders, people looking for a quick fix in a situation that offers none—looking for the unattainable because it feels more pleasing to do so, and damn the consequences. Among human transgressions, being idealistic may not rank with murder, but it is anything but noble and, in truth, far from decent.

Democratic Realities

Let us, then, set aside any careless impulse to speak of democratic ideals and speak instead of democratic realities. And let us not speak of war and peace but of that messy condition which is neither of these things and which happens to be the state of play between democratic societies and totalitarian ones.

First, as we unhappily do not need to be reminded, the number of nations even attempting to guarantee liberty to their citizens is a small one, whereas the number of nations in the grip of grim and/or bloody totalitarianism appears to grow year by year.

Second, Soviet communism has since its rise to power in Russia been an expansive, aggressive, revolutionary force, seeking by subversion, intimidation, in recent decades nuclear blackmail, and, where necessary or possible, outright military conquest, to achieve hegemony over the world.

Third, the only thing that has stood between the Soviet Union and the realization of its international ambitions has been an alliance headed by the United States and supported by the nations of Western Europe and Japan: Our alliance harbors no such imperialistic ambitions—quite the contrary—and its only *raison d'être* (and that is part of the problem) has been to arrest the spread of Soviet domination.

Fourth, that alliance is now coming unstuck. We might discuss where and how it is coming unstuck in detail, but that has been done in many other forums. Suffice it to say that the West Europeans, not without a great deal of justice, have lost faith in the capacity of the United States to play the role history has handed it, and that the Americans, with equal justice, have lost faith in the West Europeans' commitment to bearing their rightful share of what must be a common burden. The specific charges and counter-charges here are not only divisive, they are *irrelevant*. For our real problem, within ourselves and among us, lies in any case not in our respective shortcomings but in our virtues as societies.

It is not in the nature of Western democratic societies that they remain steadily and staunchly mobilized, as we are now required to do. The liberties we enjoy; the wealth and widespread well-being that only liberty seems able to produce; the notions of equity and civic propriety and private happiness that underlie our political institutions—in short, those things that rightly make us the envy of the whole world—also make us peaceable, unmilitant, and slow to act until we are threatened. There is that in Western democratic man—it is, *up to a point*, an attractive thing to say about him—which does not love to bear or use arms.

Not altogether unlike the youth of the sixties and seventies, we members of democratic societies tend to resist the dirty business that life sometimes imposes upon us. The gaudiest case of this was, of course, to be found in the 1930s, when Britain, France, and the United States, against everything they could see and hear and were actually being told, pretended to themselves that Hitler was only out to rectify a couple of his borders. This trick of self-deception is being repeated in our time in the assertion that the Soviet Union is only a nation among nations, a power among powers, seeking merely to assure its national self-interest. The purpose of this self-deception, like the self-deception of the Allies in the 1930s, is to evade the necessary and possibly politically unpopular need to arm ourselves to the teeth, draw a line, and to say to our enemy and *mean* it, "You step over that line at your grave peril."

The result of that earlier evasion was a war—a war, it may be hard to remember in the face of the condition of Western Europe today, that came perilously close to dooming our entire civilization. (Those who live in Poland, Czechoslovakia, Hungary, and East Germany, for example, would have reason to say that it *did* doom it.) The result of our present evasion, should it completely overtake the policies of our governments as it has now and then threatened to do, would be the same.

My strongly held belief is that this precious gift we call Western democracy is indivisible. This is not, unhappily, the position of all my countrymen; nor, perhaps even more unhappily, does it appear to be the position of all West Europeans. I cannot cite political, historical, or even strategic evidence for this belief: strictly speaking, there is none. But should Western Europe go down, however it may happen, by surrender or by defeat, so too would the United States. And vice versa. What sustains our societies is not only the safeguarding of our respective national interests narrowly understood but our common political, social and moral ethos. A major blow to that ethos on either side of the Atlantic will have dire consequences for the other— in demoralization, dissolution, and despair. We are too small a minority among the world's nations. We cannot spiritually survive, as we did in the 1930s, the defection of Germany, or as we did in the 1940s, the fall of France. Nor could the West Europeans survive intact the final fulfillment of the true threat to the United States contained in the fall to Soviet domination of Central and South America. Unpleasant as the thought might be to many people in the United States and Western Europe, we are stuck with one another. With those of my fellow Americans and those West Europeans who are skeptical about this proposition I can only plead: Do *not* put it to the test. We should then, too late, all find ourselves in societies restricted to that life so famously described by Thomas Hobbes as nasty, brutish, and short. And history would look back upon us and declare: Look what they had— and did not deserve to keep.

The Defense of Democratic Societies

What, then, are we, disadvantaged as I have said by our very virtues, to do at this most critical juncture of our political existence? What we must do in the first instance is something we must do to ourselves. That is, we must face and admit the cold, brutish truth about our situation. That being accomplished, we shall have far less difficulty dealing with our enemy.

What is that cold, brutal truth? Quite simply, that we are threatened, not, as the "idealists" in our respective countries have been so lustfully declaring, with the extinction of the planet, but with the collapse of our finely and delicately balanced societies beneath the weight of that advancing, ponderous barbarism called communism. Furthermore, this onslaught finds us not—*not yet*—spiritually prepared to save ourselves.

In the perspective of eternity, this is an astonishing thing to recognize. For no one any longer has the right to any illusions about communism. Those who have doomed themselves, or have been doomed by Western cupidity (or stupidity), to live under communist tyranny hate it. No matter how ugly or cruel the government replaced by it, communism has created even greater misery: more poverty, more cynicism, more murder, more despair. As Daniel P. Moynihan once observed, no one has ever climbed into a leaky boat to sail to the Soviet Union, or to Cuba, or for that matter to China. Sixty-five years of hard-won experience by millions upon millions of our utterly hopeless fellow human beings must have left us all perfectly disabused on this point. On the other side are modern Western societies whose discovery of the principle of liberty has provided their citizens not only with freedom, public and private, but with the means to create untold, undreamed of, wealth and to distribute that wealth more broadly, more equitably, than any other societies in human history. There is, as we say in the United States, no contest.

Yet there are those in our societies who ask us not to resist. Some of them, communists themselves, seek no more than to come to power. In this, they need not trouble us. Communists do not come to power by democratic means in democratic societies. The danger they represent lies only in their opportunities to poison the minds and sap the will of others. Such opportunities, however, are being plentifully provided.

They are provided, as I noted earlier, in the repetition of the noxious idea that any society falling short of utopia is not worth defending.

They are provided, far more insidiously, in the idea that international relations is a matter which concerns the behavior of nations understood as nothing more than powers acting as powers, without reference to their internal political morality. Here, of course, I am speaking of that habit of mind that goes by the name of *Realpolitik*. Adherents of *Realpolitik* will tell you that America's commitment to Western Europe at the close of World War II was merely a means of self-interested self-protection (and also, let us never forget, a means of opening up markets). Adherents of *Realpolitik* will tell you that the Soviet Union, too, has interests like any other nation and that these can be traded off, adjudicated, like those of any other nation, through diplomacy.

In the United States (and no doubt also in Western Europe) there has been a thirty-year debate, sometimes friendly, sometimes touched with asperity, between the so-called hard-headed realists and the anticommunist ideologues about the needs and purposes of Western power. The ideologues have been accused by the so-called realists of failing to understand the subtleties and flexibilities of East-West relations, of being crusaders, moralists, of bringing in principle where principle does not apply—of being, in a word, childish. But when the time came, it was the hard-headed people who created the policy of detente—a policy whose intention was to ensnare the Soviet Union in a web of international economic and political entanglements but whose real effect was, on the contrary, to entangle *us* instead. The economic, the political, the technological, not to mention the military, advantages of detente have all moved one way in the wrong direction; at every juncture, we discovered there was to be no *quo* for the *quid*. The debate has been settled. To be an anticommunist ideologue is precisely to be in the position to provide far better, far more practical, hard-headed, serviceable advice about how to understand and deal with the Soviet Union than all the accumulated wisdoms of ordinary statecraft.

All this aside, it is these voices of so-called hard-headedness among us that help to undermine our capacity to face the hard and brutal truth and that provide the richest opportunities of all for those who seek our downfall. Ronald Reagan's use of the simple (*not* simplistic) word "evil" in speaking of the Soviet Union was salutary. Had it not been, neither the Soviets nor the Western press would have been so agitated by it. For in the face of such a word, one is obligated to *do* something: to rouse oneself, to mobilize, and to remain ever alert. It is not the Ronald Reagan who speaks of good and evil who threatens the peace of the world. It is the Ronald Reagan who succumbs to the abuse of the peaceniks, the stridency of the world press, the contempt of the "realpolitikers", and the cheap anxieties of his political counsellors and sends his minions to pursue the fruitless expedient of arms control—it is this Ronald Reagan who threatens the peace of the world.

The democratic West, though presently hampered by its reluctance to make hard choices, is far from helpless. We possess that greatest of all assets, a healthy and productive populace. If our elites are decadent—and they are: whose children, after all, march in the streets of Bonn and London and New York demanding our surrender?—our ordinary citizens are not. Our economies, to the extent that they remain free, cannot only out-produce and out-distribute all others; they can also be vibrantly responsive to new demands, to innovation, to the need for moving quickly. Our political institutions, despite all the careless pressure we have put upon them in recent years, are sound. If guns, missiles, planes, tanks, and armies must be maintained in a state of readiness to protect us and to keep the peace, we can admit them to our national lives without fear of corruption. They are costly and inconvenient, to be sure, but they are *not* ignoble.

When we speak of democratic ideals, *true* democratic ideals, we would do well to subsume them all under one emblazoned statement: "The alternative is simply unacceptable." The alternative is unacceptable to us, to those who must languish under it, and to those who will come after us.

"The tree of liberty," it was once long ago said, "is watered by the blood of martyrs." We have no right, and we have no *need*, to let the precious legacy left us by those martyrs—through our own blindness and trembling, and with no thought for the future—slip through our fingers.

Arms Control and Morality

by Pierre Hassner

"WITH THE CHAMPIONS of faith, no dialogue is possible." This remark by Max Weber, quoted by Karl Jaspers in his book, *The Atomic Bomb and the Future of Mankind*, can have many different meanings.[1] It can be understood to apply to religious faith proper, or to political positions based on an absolute moral or mystical stand, or even to a "secular religion" like Marxism. It may be taken to deny that a non-believer, who tries to apply rational criteria to political matters, can legitimately engage in a dialogue with Christian churches about nuclear weapons, or, for that matter, that he can even engage in a meaningful debate with antinuclear activists, whether they be followers of the Sermon on the Mount, seekers of the absolute purity of the soul, or merely secular devotees of Weberian ethics.[2] In a completely different sense, moreover, it can be taken to deny that meaningful negotiations on arms control are possible with leaders of a power like the Soviet Union whose outlook, objectives, and values are based on a combination of Leninist and Russian historical traditions.

In each of the cases, the validity of Max Weber's dictum is suspect. I maintain that there still exists a minimum of common interests even among enemy states. I believe, moreover, that the potential exists for maintaining a common language based on rationality, even among cultural and ideological strangers. This attempt at a dialogue, however, can be meaningful only if the basic differences in assumptions and attitudes, as well as goals and principles, are not glossed over.[3]

One of the crucial aspects of detente, of course, has been the interconnected themes of arms control and morality. In a sense one might be justified in wondering why the connection between these two particular terms has been singled out in the first place. After all, while the question of the morality of war, and even of nuclear deterrence, is an obvious and inevitable one, arms control as such, *if it works*, would seem to be as unobjectionable as motherhood and early spring. The real question about it is whether it is realistic, or whether the primacy of political conflict and the influence of strategic constraints are such as to make it an illusion, and a dangerous

---

[1] Karl Jaspers, *La Bombe Atomique et l'Avenir de l'Homme* (Paris: Buchet-Chastel, 1963), p. 5. The original German edition was *Die Atombombe und die Zukunft des Menschen* (Munich: Piper, 1958).

[2] See Franz Alt, *Frieden ist möglich: Die Politik der Bergpredigt* (Munich: Piper, 1983), and H.E. Bahr, editor, *Franziskus in Gorleben* (Frankfurt: Fischer, 1981).

[3] Jaspers, *op. cit.*, p. 515.

one at that, if one side shows restraint while the other exploits the arms control process for unilateral gains.

Hence, the answer to our question would seem to rely entirely upon specific judgments not only about the nature of nuclear deterrence and the arms race but about the nature of communist regimes and of the East-West confrontation as well. Arms control and morality would both seem to lie in a kind of abstract vacuum as long as they are not given a substantive content by political and military assumptions.

Yet some assumptions—both political and military—are inseparable from the notion of arms control as such. The first is, precisely, the need for control over arms. This means the primacy of politics. But it also means that, if it is to be effective, arms policy must consist neither in total unilateral disarmament nor in total military victory through unrestrained warfare. The structure of an international system divided into independent states and the nature of nuclear weapons are supposed to make the two extreme solutions impossible. Necessity, self-interest, or the common interest of the planet would seem to call for a politics based on the two most universal moral imperatives: self-restraint and reciprocity. Yet, considering these imperatives as practical guidelines for making foreign policy inevitably raises other questions, both technical and political. Does the nature of nuclear weapons (in terms of their deadliness and of the likelihood of escalation), for example, allow for their restrained use? Does the nature of communications and, hence, the limits of our knowledge about the other side's capabilities, intentions and actions, allow for reciprocity, whether in arms developments or in crisis, let alone war? Or is unilateral renunciation the only way out? Conversely, does not the nature of the political enemy make his own restraint or acceptance of a common language, let alone of common rules of the game, unlikely? And in this case does it make sense to act with restraint toward an unrestrained enemy, to try to carry on a dialogue with someone whose *modus operandi* is one of deceit? Or is the unilateral pursuit of security through strength the only way out?

These questions, arising from both technical and political considerations, strike at the very heart of the larger question of whether it is possible to reconcile arms control and morality in the nuclear age. They force us to reveal the assumptions underlying our conceptions of morality, arms control, military technology, and political strategy.

What Kind of Morality?

One advantage of the current unholy mixture of theology and strategy brought about by the nuclear debate is that it forces the political and arms control analyst to be specific about his fundamental philosophical premises. This is neither entirely natural nor necessarily advisable: All political life is predicated upon certain unspoken assumptions which, if the community is to remain intact, cannot be called into question by any citizen. Yet, in extreme situations the Judeo-Christian tradition on which our morality is based (whether religiously inspired or simply cultural) calls for the individual conscience to make its own judgment, and even more importantly, to take its own stand. The question, then, is first, whether the gravity of the issue makes the choice any less complex; second, whether the danger of nuclear war is one of those extreme situations which calls for radical moral choice; and, third—and in my view most importantly—what is the nature of the relationship, in theory and practice, between the extreme existential situation and the normal political one?

All three questions will be answered differently according to one's moral code and according to one's interpretation of the facts. For instance, the American bishops take an unequivocally negative attitude (based on Vatican II) toward countercity deterrence even when used as a threat of retaliation after a nuclear attack. They take a more qualified yet still firmly negative view of the possibilities of limiting, controlling, and discriminating between nuclear weapons, a stand which implies strategic and technical assumptions which may be right or wrong, but which nonetheless are certainly debatable and have been challenged by authorities at least as competent as those on which they rely. Finally, they draw a distinction between the possession of nuclear weapons and the threat to use them; and they imply a belief that nuclear deterrence is compatible with a declared intention of not using nuclear weapons, which is highly debatable not only from the point of view of moral theology but from that of deterrent psychology and political prudence as well.

It seems fair, then, to state that unless one takes the two extreme positions of either unconditionally forbidding the use of force or pursuing self-interest without due regard to moral considerations (which can lead either to a Hobbesian primacy of the fear of violent death or to the abandonment of any restraint in the violent pursuit of power), one is inevitably embarked upon a course that will lead to questions of politics and strategy which have no simple or unambiguous answers. The slogan "better red than dead" rather confuses the issue, and the commonsensical answer "neither red nor dead" begs the question. One can opt for neither before asking whose survival is being assured, what is meant by "red," and whether the issue is not that of survival but rather that of murder. In other words, is not the question whether it is better to submit to injustice than to commit it, or to be either dead or red than murderer? This in turn raises the question: murderer of whom? The character both of totalitarian regimes (which make it more desirable than ever to distinguish between rulers and ruled) and of modern weapons (which so far have made this distinction more difficult to discern than ever before) raises this last issue with particular poignancy.

Whether one thinks in terms of survival or of retaliation, a further unsolved and unsolvable issue is that of numbers.[4] It is easy enough for almost all believers in the dignity of man to agree that it is based on placing a higher value on freedom than on one's own physical survival. Does this change when one commits one's fellow citizens? Or when the survival of hundreds of millions is at stake? Or that of the whole human race? Is the moral problem of killing millions of combatants in defense or in retaliation, and additional tens of millions of noncombatants through unavoidable collateral effects, different from holding hundreds of millions of people as hostages?

All these problems are *ultimately* unresolvable on the moral level for any one who does not base his stand on divine inspiration. But prudential and provisional solutions—which depend upon assumptions regarding such matters as the credibility of deterrence and the possibility of discrimination and control, and which can mitigate the dilemmas—while highly speculative, are nevertheless subject to factual analysis.

Nobody has formulated the most basic dilemma with greater care and precision than the German philosopher Karl Jaspers. In his important book, *The Atomic Bomb and the Future of Mankind*, written a quarter of a century ago, Jaspers draws a parallel between two fundamental risks: "The atom bomb would probably, although not certainly, destroy all life on earth. To be deprived of one's liberty by totalitarianism would deprive life of all value, even though it is not certain that it would last forever."[5] "In all these arguments for and against the ultimate risk, one should not forget that both sides count upon a certainty which does not exist: no option has the destruction of mankind or the degradation of the value of its life as a certain consequence. No situation is absolutely hopeless."[6] It is in this margin for hope that morality and arms control can meet. But the question is how?

The usual way in which the basic dilemma is posed is in terms of Max Weber's distinction between the ethics of conviction and the ethics of responsibility. This is, for instance, the case in the Federal Republic, in the debate between Franz Alt, a Christian journalist who calls for the politics of the Sermon on the Mount, and Manfred Hattich, a political scientist who believes that peace is achieved not by moral intentions but by exercising political responsibility.[7] Yet, while the latter obviously has the better of the argument, the Weberian distinction as such is of limited value for several reasons. First, Weber himself pointed out that these two ethical standpoints have to be combined: the responsible man must in some extreme cases take

---

[4] See the discussion by Robert W. Tucker, "The Moral Economy of Force," in Robert E. Osgood and Robert W. Tucker, editors, *Force, Order and Justice* (Baltimore, Md.: The Johns Hopkins Press, 1967), pp. 248-323.

[5] Jaspers, *op. cit.*, p. 311.

[6] *Ibid.*, p. 306.

[7] Manfred Hattich, *Weltfrieden durch Friedfertigkeit?* (Munich: Olzog, 1983).

an absolute moral stand, just as the proponent of moral purity cannot ignore political consequences if he wants to influence politics at all. Second, in the current debate, the tables can easily be turned. The ethics of conviction may lead to unconditional resistance to aggression, while the ethics of responsibility may lead to concern with the fate of the planet. Third, the distinction itself is to some extent artificial.

Any moral intention, if it is serious, has to consider the consequences of the intended action; any moral judgment concerning the actual consequences of an action, on the other hand, has to consider whether such consequences were intended or unforeseeable, or whether they were foreseeable but insufficiently taken into account. There remains, however, a possible gap between the exigencies of the individual conscience and those of the state. This gap can become dramatic and perhaps even irrevocable in an extreme situation. But the essence of the problem is to prevent such an extreme situation from arising, while nevertheless facing up to its ultimate possibility. It is precisely this dialectical interplay between normal and extreme situations that the political ethics of Aristotle—particularly as reinterpreted by Leo Strauss[8]—and the existential ethics of Karl Jaspers are addressing far more seriously than either the "idealist" or "realist" positions in the current debate over nuclear strategy.

Strauss defines an extreme situation as one

in which the very existence or independence of a society is at stake. In such a situation, and only in such a situation, can it justly be said that the public safety is the highest law. A decent society will not go to war except for a just cause. But what it will do during a war will depend to a certain extent on what the enemy—possibly an absolutely unscrupulous and savage enemy—forces it to do. There are no limits which can be defined in advance; there are no assignable limits to what might become just reprisals. In extreme situations the normally valid rules of natural law are justly changed, or changed in accordance with natural law; the exceptions are as just as the law itself.

Aristotle seems to suggest that there is not a single rule, however basic, which is not subject to exception. Justice has two different principles or sets of principles: the requirements of public safety, or what is necessary in extreme situations to preserve the existence or independence of society on the one hand, and the rules of justice in a more precise sense on the other. And there is no principle that defines clearly in what types of cases the public safety, and in what types of cases the precise rules of justice have priority, for it is not possible to define precisely what constitutes an extreme as opposed to a normal situation. Every dangerous external or internal enemy is capable of transforming what can reasonably be regarded as a normal situation into an extreme one. Natural law must be mutable in order to cope with the multifarious forms of wickedness. What cannot be decided in advance by universal rules, what can be decided at the critical moment by the most competent and most conscientious statesman on the scene, can be made to appear as just in

---

[8] Leo Strauss, *Natural Right and History* (Chicago, Ill.: University of Chicago Press, 1953), pp. 160-162.

retrospect; the objective discrimination between extreme actions which were just and extreme actions which were unjust is one of the noblest duties of the historian.[9]

Of course, this may seem to be an extremely loose distinction, leaving maximum freedom for the statesman to act and for the historian to justify him after the fact. But Strauss adds:

It is important that the difference between the Aristotelian view of natural law and Machiavellianism be clearly understood. Machiavelli denies natural law because he takes his bearings from extreme situations in which the demands of justice are reduced to the requirements of necessity and not from normal situations in which the demands of justice are strictly the highest law. The true statesman, in the Aristotelian sense, takes his bearings from the normal situation and from what is normally right, and he reluctantly deviates from this course only in order to save the cause of justice and humanity itself. No legal expression of this difference can be found. Its political importance is obvious. The two opposite extremes, which are at present called "cynicism" and "idealism," combine in order to blur this difference. And, as everyone can see, they have not been unsuccessful.[10]

While the Straussian-Aristotelian position is essentially rationalistic and biased in favor of the political and the normal, Jaspers puts more stress on the existential, the individual, and the extreme. Whereas for Strauss, the extreme situation has to be seen in light of the normal one, for Jaspers every normal decision, even the smallest one, has to be seen in light of the extreme situation.[11] In our case, the extreme situation—the risk of physical destruction of the planet by nuclear weapons or of spiritual destruction through totalitarianism—transcends the political dimension. It is one of those ultimate *Grenzsituationen*—pivotal situations like death, conflict, sacrifice—which give existence its meaning. The responsibility it calls for is not simply that of the statesman toward the common good but of the individual toward the meaning of existence. Hence, while Strauss would suggest that every extreme situation has a just solution in principle, or retrospectively, but one that cannot be spelled out in advance, Jaspers would tend to think in terms of an existential gamble from which, even retrospectively, one cannot eliminate the elements of freedom and uncertainty.

In practical terms, however, what unites both positions seems to me more important than what divides them. Both agree on the impossibility of making decisions for the extreme situation in advance. Moreover, they agree that it is our duty to prevent the extreme situation from arising and, for this reason, to balance the just and the necessary, the imperatives of survival and dignity, and the exigencies of a particular situation and ultimate moral

---

[9] *Ibid.*, p. 161.
[10] *Ibid.*, p. 162.
[11] Jaspers, *op. cit.*, p. 435.

principles. Both warn against the twin dangers of idealism and cynicism, against behaving as if the extreme situation were never to arise or as if it were already present.[12] They agree that the only conceivable way to avoid any risk would be to sacrifice one of the vital imperatives and that in fact this would only increase the risk of jeopardizing both. As far as arms control is concerned, both would claim that restraint and dialogue are always desirable but not always possible, that the real test emerges when one is faced with an unrestrained and deceitful enemy, when one is forced to answer the question, as formulated by Jaspers: "How can one talk with totalitarians?"[13] Dealing with totalitarians involves both firmness and openness, both the need to maintain the balance and the need to maintain communications, both the attempt to reach the people beyond the system and the need not to forget the system. One could put it in religious terms, by saying that to love one's enemy in politics means to love him without forgetting that, in terms of systems if not of individuals, he is still an enemy.

Ultimately, Strauss and Jaspers point toward a political conception of the problem of peace, both in its strategic and in its moral dimensions, such as has been advocated by two Germans, the Protestant theologian Trutz Rendtorff and the Christian Democratic politician Alois Mertes.[14] A real peace ethic cannot stop at a consideration of the weapons involved, any more than a meaningful strategy for defense and arms control can. It must consider the structure of political conflicts and the political implications of military and arms control postures. It must recognize existing asymmetries in political regimes and objectives, yet aim, by putting military and negotiating strategies at the service of long-term political goals, to build structures and to encourage changes which may lead from a minimum of reciprocity based on mutual interest in survival to a genuine reciprocity based on political reconciliation.

What Kind of Arms Control?

The implications for arms control in a more precise sense should be clear enough. They happen to converge with the lessons this writer draws from past efforts at negotiation.

---

[12] *Ibid.*, p. 673.
[13] *Ibid.*, p. 458.
[14] Trutz Rendtorff, "Friedensethik—ein Weg zur Wiederentdeckung der politischen Struktur militärischer Rüstung," in Uwe Nerlich, editor, *Sowjetische Macht und Westliche Verhandlungspolitik im Wandel militärischer Kräfteverhältnisse* (Baden-Baden: Nomos, 1982), pp. 541-559; and Alois Mertes, "Friedenserhaltung-Friedensgestaltung: Zur Diskussion über 'Sicherheitspartnerschaft,'" *Europa-Archiv*, No. 7, April 10, 1983, pp. 187-196.

Let us start from where morality and arms control meet—namely, at the point of juncture of *restraint* and *reciprocity*. The principle of restraint does not lead to the banning of any weapon as intrinsically bad, or even to the unconditional forbidding of any action—given the unpredictability of where the tragic dilemmas of an extreme situation may lead. But it does call (along with the just war principles of proportionality and discrimination) for limiting the amount of suffering and destruction to a degree that is compatible with legitimate military and political goals. Conversely, if the latter is defined, in Jaspers' terms, as preventing both the extension of totalitarianism and the destruction of the planet, there is a mutual relationship between goals and means: The danger of blowing up the planet with the existing means of destruction restricts the scope for a just war and thereby demands a more modest and defensive definition of goals in the struggle against totalitarianism. Thus, the very nature of the goal requires restraint in the means utilized to achieve it; it requires not only discrimination between populations, military forces, and leaders, but avoidance of nuclear escalation. This dual goal of ensuring survival *and* freedom may or may not create difficult dilemmas in terms of deterrence, but it will certainly not allow for any simple solution. However, it does strengthen a *prima facie* case for deterrence by denial as opposed to deterrence by retaliation, for a policy of "no launch on warning," and for a posture that does not make an early use of nuclear weapons inevitable. Moreover, it strengthens the case, if deterrence fails, for avoiding not only the targeting of the enemy's top leadership whose restraint one would want to encourage, but also the indiscriminate destruction of populations. Hence, it would militate in favor both of limited nuclear options and of civil and active defense, if and when they are technically possible.

These are precepts geared more to strategic than to negotiating postures. But they suggest that it is imperative that arms control proposals at least not make restraint more difficult, which is certainly what happens when one promotes nuclear-free zones or identifies stability with mutually assured destruction. Second, to the extent that the precepts discussed above tend to lead one to favor counterforce and active defense policies, and hence may be interpreted as leading to an offensive strategy and an unlimited arms race, it becomes all the more necessary to embrace the arms control process and to communicate assurances to the enemy in areas such as targeting. Such a perspective may end up being strategically the least unstable and morally the least unsatisfactory; it may end up in an arms control regime based on mutual assured survival, i.e., on coupling anti-missile defense with reductions in offensive weapons, as suggested by the late Donald Brennan.

Of course, all this depends to a great extent upon how far one can go in the second direction, that of reciprocity. Here both ethics and politics teach us to distinguish between, first, the illusions of what Father James

V. Schall calls an "ideology of dialogue"; second, the technical necessities of tacit or explicit bargaining, even in situations of asymmetry and conflict; and, third, the desirable search for political reciprocity.[15]

Dialogue seen as an end in itself is not to be rejected out of hand, for it does respond to the genuine need for the two superpowers to communicate and to be seen as doing so. But it can be dangerous if it means agreement for agreement's sake, if the realities of asymmetry and conflict are ignored, and, in particular, if communication becomes an instrument for disguising one's intentions as much as for revealing them. Besides, breaking communications may in itself—if it is limited in time and in scope—sometimes be a useful political tactic. Asymmetry and uncertainty render the notions of general disarmament and "an end to the arms race" utopian and dangerous. Arms control in the strong, maximalist sense would be possible only under conditions of verification which are certainly prohibited by the nature of the Soviet regime and probably by that of the international system.

But this does not detract in the least from the fact that deterrence and arms control, while not being a purely cooperative game (as implied by arms control ideologists in the United States and, more recently, in the Federal Republic with such notions as *Kooperative Rüstungssteuerung*—cooperative arms control—and *Sicherheitspartnershaft*—security partnership—have implied), are nevertheless non-zero-sum games involving both conflict and cooperation.[16] Even among basically different and conflicting rivals common interests do exist, although it is hard to acknowledge them and to bring them into the bargaining process in the absence of a common code. Hence, the search for common rules, based on balance and self-interest and, more often than not, on provisional abstention from certain weapons systems or certain areas of conflict (after all, even Hitler tacitly recognized the need for reciprocal arms control by observing the ban on gas warfare), is of the utmost importance.

Finally, in the long run, moral, security, and political considerations converge to make it desirable to use arms control to promote modest transformations in the Soviet Union (by reducing secrecy, improving verification, complicating the use of force against other communist countries as well as against the West and the nonaligned) and to encourage a more genuine reciprocity. Confidence-building measures, more than arms reductions, may contribute to this goal.

At any rate, while from a security point of view the most important arms control measures may be unilateral, from a political point of view it is essential

---

[15] Father James V. Schall in "Morality and Deterrence: Albert Wohlstetter and Critics," *Commentary*, December 1983, p. 8.
[16] See the critique by Mertes, *op. cit.*

to uphold the long-range goal of reciprocity as the only basis for genuine stability, and to recognize the primacy of balance and deterrence as long as reciprocity is absent. It is just as essential to accustom ourselves to the idea that while an immense gap exists between current realities and the best international regime, it is still true, to paraphrase Paul Ramsey, that today's world is not one of "illimitable animosity," and that tomorrow's world, as long as it is still the city of man and not the city of God, cannot be a pure "trust system."[17] Today we are and shall remain living in "systems of distrust" so long as our's is a world of sovereign states. But we can move from a world of opposing systems into a world of competing ones; and even within the world of opposing systems—which is unavoidable so long as the basic opposition between freedom and totalitarianism is compounded by the fundamental distrust among sovereign states—deterrence and arms control can serve to transform a more distrustful, intense, and dangerous opposition into a more patient, controlled, and secure one.

What Kind of Technology?

Not only this kind of historical perspective or the debate over arms control, but even the most abstract and absolute ethical or theological judgments put forth in the present nuclear debate (in particular by the American bishops and by their opponents)—all rely heavily on assumptions about technology. Obviously my own judgments are no exception. What distinguishes me from some other participants in the debate is perhaps my awareness, first, of my own limited competence in technological matters and of the objective uncertainties involved, and, second, of the natural bias I share with every one else for choosing technical conclusions which conform to my particular moral and political preferences. Clearly, much of what I have said so far is more in line with the minority of strategists headed by Albert Wohlstetter.[18] These strategists believe that the progress of precision and control gives us more freedom to choose proportionally restrained and discriminating responses, which are, in my opinion, more credible and more moral than those advocated by the American bishops, for whom nuclear war is by definition uncontrollable and the progress of technology serves only to create more illusions, fears, temptations, and instability. Similarly, I tend to side with that minority of theologians who believe, with James Turner Johnson, that enhanced radiation weapons are a positive step toward resolving our dilemma, because they reduce collateral damage, favor deter-

---

[17] Paul Ramsey, "A Political Ethics Context for Strategic Thinking," in Morton A. Kaplan, editor, *Strategic Thinking and Its Moral Implications* (Chicago, Ill.: University of Chicago Press, 1973), pp. 108-112.
[18] See, above all, Albert Wohlstetter, "Bishops, Statesmen and Other Strategists on Bombing Innocents," *Commentary*, June 1983, and the discussion with his critics in *Commentary*, December 1983.

rence by denial, and discriminate between combatants and noncombatants.[19] Finally, I agree with a minority of arms controllers who, like the late Donald Brennan, maintain that the Antiballistic Missile Treaty (ABM), while being so far one of the most tangible results ever to come out of arms control negotiations, may very well have been a step backward in the search for a livable world.

On all of these issues, however, my prevalent feeling is one of uncertainty. For instance, regarding the possibility of limited and controllable nuclear war, I tend to think that Wohlstetter has the better technological argument, but I nonetheless believe that human factors are likely to contribute to confusion and uncontrollable escalation in a major war, as his opponents argue. As far as President Reagan's "star wars" speech is concerned, I tend to be at least as impressed by the overwhelming weight of technical opinion stressing the difficulties and dangers of such an undertaking as I am by its desirability if it were successful. On deterrence by local denial, I see no serious objection, but only so long as it is not shaped in such a way as to diminish the residual credibility of escalation, which remains a basic element at least of "extended deterrence."

How, then, can one base immediate decisions, long-range strategies, and permanent moral attitudes upon such a shaky ground as that of untested existing technologies and debatable future ones? I believe two distinctions are crucial, although like all dilemmas of the nuclear age, they become absurd if pushed to an extreme.

The first distinction is between existing realities and models for the future. For the present, I agree with Keeny and Panofsky, who insist that the mutual hostage relationship is currently the basis of deterrence and hence of security, but for the long run I agree with Fred Iklé, who asks whether nuclear deterrence can last out the century.[20] Neither the proponents of limitation and control, of active defense, or of conventional postures have convinced me that the risk of escalation to mutual suicide is not the ultimate basis for peace, or, for that matter, that it could ever be eliminated as an extreme possibility. But nothing of what the proponents of the doctrine of Mutual Assured Destruction (MAD) have to say convinces me that basing the world's security primarily on the threat of suicide and genocide is an ideal defense model, or even the only conceivable one. In my opinion, the credibility and acceptability of the MAD doctrine are rapidly declining: It is imperative to think of other models which would remove the mutual hostage relationship from

---

[19] James Turner Johnson, *Just War Tradition and the Restraint of War* (Princeton, N.J.: Princeton University Press, 1981), pp. 365-366; his contribution to the Wohlstetter discussion in *Commentary*, December 1983; and his new book, *Can Modern War Be Just?* (New Haven, Conn.: Yale University Press, 1984).

[20] Spurgeon M. Keeny, Jr., and Wolfgang K.H. Panofsky, "MAD versus NUTS: Can Doctrine or Weaponry Remedy the Mutual Hostage Relationship of the Superpowers?," *Foreign Affairs*, Winter 1981/82, pp. 287-304; and Fred Iklé, "Can Nuclear Deterrence Last Out the Century?," *Foreign Affairs*, January 1973, pp. 267-285.

the forefront of our thinking and planning (where a mixture of technological necessity and of intellectual and moral laziness have put it for a number of decades) and place it in the background where it will remain an unwanted but always possible alternative if all other defense strategies fail.

Perhaps our greatest challenge is how to articulate, on the one hand, the transient and permanent structural components of security such as the balance of power and nuclear deterrence, and, on the other hand, if deterrence fails, the need for restraint and damage-limitation in the face of changing and uncertain risks and opportunities spawned by a dynamic technology. This effort is probably endangered equally by those who, like the proponents of the nuclear freeze, oppose new technological developments that may increase our chances for maintaining a more credible and humane posture, and by those who, by over-selling these technologies, create the illusion that we already have credible alternatives to countercity deterrence and who, therefore, may both weaken deterrence and create fears of an easier resort to limited war.

This leads us to a second distinction I would like to make, a distinction between the various uses of new technologies. The entire debate over new technologies is obscured by the polarization between those who tend to present any new technology as destabilizing and those who, conversely, seem to believe that ever-increasing sophistication necessarily means ever-increasing security. Of course, this polarization has some ground in reality. Precisely because the performances and prospects of each individual system are so debatable, one probably needs a global choice for or against the search for new technologies. If the choice is put in such terms, it would have to go against the believers in a technological plateau or the supporters of a nuclear freeze. But this should not blind us to a kernel of truth in their arguments, that, for example, the dangers of surprise attack grow along with increases in accuracy.

Of course, a world based on the mutual invulnerability of strategic forces and on the mutual vulnerability of populations is a mad world. But a world based on great differentials in the vulnerability of strategic forces and populations is madder still. To encourage the Soviets to make their forces invulnerable to the very strikes whose effectiveness the United States was seeking to improve was a contradictory policy inspired by what John Erickson has called "the chimera of mutual deterrence."[21] Certainly the Soviets, given their ideology, must have thought so, and only the particular ideological blindness of orthodox arms controllers can take Soviet charges seriously that any new Western system, whether it be the enhanced radiation warhead or the cruise missile, is inherently destabilizing and aggressive.

---

[21] John Erickson, "The Chimera of Mutual Deterrence," *Strategic Review*, Spring 1978, pp. 11-17.

But the reasoning that any system which the Soviets and "freezeniks" hate cannot be all bad is itself somewhat dangerous. The habit of constantly "crying wolf" without justification does not necessarily mean that the Soviets are not genuinely fearful of future American first-strike capabilities or of genuine temptations to preempt. The same weapons systems (for example, partially vulnerable land-based theater nuclear weapons in Europe), which contribute to extended deterrence because of their recoupling effect (since the Soviets would have to eliminate them and, for this very reason, force the United States to use them quickly), may, because of the same "use them or lose them" effect, be bad for crisis stability.

A coherent arms policy—inspired by political and arms control considerations—which aims at improving flexibility and control without putting an increasing premium on surprise and deception would have to encourage some technological developments and discourage others. Moreover, it would have to resort to declaratory or arms control measures in order to minimize the damage coming from the inevitable trade-offs between military and political security.

Nothing may be more utopian, given the competing "mad momenta" of technology and arms control, than this kind of delicate political steering between opposite dangers. But if the dilemmas, ambiguities, and contradictions of our nuclear and divided world are genuine, it is still better to try to master them, however unsuccessfully, than either to ignore them or, by over-dramatizing them, to keep switching from one extreme to the other.

What Kind of Strategy?

We started by affirming the role of politics in managing the dilemmas of morality and arms control. We end by affirming its role in managing the dilemmas of deterrence and defense. This is true, first, because only a political strategy (inspired by the imperatives of morality and informed by the constraints of security) can provide the overarching framework capable of integrating the various dimensions of the problem, and, second, because international politics should be recognized as an immediate priority.

Many American strategists seem preoccupied above all with prevailing and damage-limitation in war-fighting strategies, and with intra-war deterrence. Many in the peace movement, on the other hand, seem preoccupied above all with the dangers associated with the outbreak of war, the moderate ones emphasizing pure deterrence and arms control and the radical ones unilateral disarmament. Both preoccupations are legitimate, but in the current debate over East-West relations, U.S.-West European ties, and long-range theater nuclear forces, the crucial element is a struggle for peacetime political influence and stability, or to put it more dramatically, a struggle for the soul of the Europeans, particularly of the Germans, and for the political domination of the continent. Certainly the more likely and more urgent danger facing Europe is, to use the current jargon, that of "Finlandization" of Western Europe and of "decoupling" it from the United States, rather than that of war. There seems little doubt that both the SS-20 and the Pershing II and cruise missiles are above all political weapons, adopted for peace-time influence more than for their operational military necessity. But if this is so, declarations and perceptions concerning the weapons are as important as the weapons themselves.

While especially valid in this particular case, the importance of political perceptions extends to the whole field of deterrence and arms control, and above all to extended deterrence. After all, a relationship of extended deterrence involves three actors, he who is threatening, the threatened, and the protector. In Europe, the debate is really not so much about what the United States would do in case of a Soviet attack against Western Europe, nor even about what the Soviets think the United States would do, but rather about what the Germans think the Soviets will think the Americans will do. The three functions of nuclear weapons (defense, deterrence, and peace-time influence) have been recognized for a long time. Michael Howard has done a real service in pointing out that the third function includes reassurance of one's own population.[22] It seems reasonable to add that in extended deterrence, this function of "reassurance" becomes both more complicated and even more important since what reassures the Americans does not necessarily reassure the Germans, who have to rely for reassurance upon a government whose interests, or at least whose perceptions, do not necessarily coincide with their own.

The dilemmas of political, peace-time reassurance versus operational, war-time effectiveness go a long way toward explaining why France has so far been spared a real pacifist movement, while the efforts of American statesmen to re-establish the credibility of deterrence have tended, in general, to frighten their own population, and even more that of their European allies. Pierre Lellouche has observed—in exaggerated but illuminating terms—that the social acceptability of a defense posture is universally proportional to its operational credibility.[23] The more the United States stresses credibility, proportionality, limitation, and control, the more it gives its allies the impression that it seriously contemplates waging a war whose costs are deemed to be tolerable. Conversely, "deterrence only" postures, whether in the form of minimum deterrence or massive retaliation, are more acceptable because they do not force widespread attention on the possibility of deterrence failing and war actually taking place. The French doctrine,

---

[22] Michael Howard, "Reassurance and Deterrence: Western Defense in the 1980s," *Foreign Affairs*, Winter 1982/83, pp. 304-324.

[23] See Pierre Lellouche, *Pacifisme et Dissuasion* (Paris: Institut Français des Relations Internationales, 1983), especially the Introduction and my chapter, "Pacifisme et Terreur."

however implausible, is tolerated precisely because of its abstractness and ambiguity, or even, for some, because of its lack of credibility. In a sense, the French position is not so far from the "existential deterrence" of the American bishops; short of unilateral disarmament, the best way to convince one's own population that going to war is not taken lightly is to have a suicidal posture. Whether this is a responsible posture to have, if one begins to take seriously the danger of deterrence failing, is another matter.

What is important to stress is that the most technically appealing and militarily (or even morally) imperative postures (be it nuclear defense or conventional offense, controlled-nuclear war or conventional second-echelon interdiction) can be disastrous if they are not part of a persuasive political package, which takes into account, for instance, both the suspicions created by the geographical discontinuity of the Atlantic Alliance and the constraints imposed by the geographical and human contiguity between the two German states.

But politics enters into even the ultimate question of deterrence itself. While it seems beyond question that the American approach is stronger on defense than on reassurance, and the French one the other way round, neither really knows how its posture looks to the Soviet side. For, while it is both militarily and morally impossible to be concerned with deterrence without considering what one would do if it failed, and while, as we have argued, peace-time influence over populations is essential, the ultimate test of nuclear deterrence is whether the potential aggressor is himself deterred. Here political considerations intervene to the extent that, contrary to abstract deterrent and arms control theory, deterrence may work differently according to the opponent's values and sense of legitimacy, which may affect his respective evaluations of human life versus political power, or his sense of the fragility of his own society and its ability to sustain a prolonged confrontation.

Still, some universal dilemmas are inescapable and unanswered. The central one which Laurence Martin has called "the dilemma of plausibility and horror" is at the root of the conflict between massive retaliation and flexible response. Does a less frightening threat have more deterrent power than a less likely but more destructive one? Common sense would seem to indicate that there must be an optimum solution where the right combination between the magnitude of the threat and its credibility is reached. Yet it is remarkable how the discussion is dominated by the two extreme positions, one of which totally eliminates the problem of credibility by radically separating deterrence from defense, while the other puts credibility so much at the center that it allows for no distinction between a deterrent and a war-fighting posture.

For a large coalition, including most arms controllers, the more moderate wing of the peace movement, the American bishops, and the advocates of

45

the orthodox French position, deterrence is acceptable so long as it is not credible. Any attempt at providing an effective defense is a sin against deterrence. This position raises problems of credibility and morality if deterrence fails.

At the other extreme, most thoroughly articulated by Wohlstetter, deterrence appears to be a mere by-product of an effective defense posture. There should be no distinction between threats *ex ante* and what one should actually be prepared to do *ex post*. This is certainly the sanest position if deterrence fails, but it raises problems with respect not only to reassurance but to deterrence as well, particularly extended deterrence. It tends to devalue the threat of involuntary escalation which may well have had something to do with the fact that so far the nuclear taboo has been respected while conventional wars have kept proliferating. It tends to maximize the freedom of action of the protector while, especially in a situation characterized by what I have called elsewhere the "mutual fear of decoupling," the protected will be reassured only by some form of commitment or hostage situation which restricts the freedom to disengage.[24] Both for the opponent and the ally, Schelling's formulation about deterrence being based less on the rationality of a decision than on the unpredictability of a process is all the more true in a time of strategic parity and intra-alliance distrust.

This is why it seems to me that, both politically and strategically, the two more complex positions are more satisfactory. One consists of threatening massive retaliation or automatic escalation, yet preparing for control, discrimination and limitation if deterrence fails. This was the position advocated by General Beaufre and, according to Nathan Leites, it is the real position of the Soviets.[25] But it implies a gap between one's declaratory policy and one's effective posture that is hard to maintain, especially for an open and democratic society like the United States.

Advocates of another position hold that deterrence should be rational, credible, and correspond to what one actually intends to do—and is prepared to do—if deterrence fails. But at the same time one should communicate to one's own population, allies, and enemies that, while one will always try for the lower and more humane response, both the magnitude of the stakes in an extreme situation and the difficulties of control may lead—especially if the other side does not observe similar restraints—to an escalation that would bring ultimate disaster for both sides. This is a position which Wohlstetter calls "Madcap."[26] He attributes it to one phase in Robert McNamara's

---

[24] Pierre Hassner, "Who is Decoupling From Whom?, or This Time, the Wolf is Here," in Lawrence S. Hagen, editor, *The Crisis in Western Security* (London: Croom Helm, 1982), pp. 168-186.
[25] Andre Beaufre, *Dissuasion et Stratégie* (Paris: Armand Colin, 1964), pp. 43-45, and Nathan Leites, *Soviet Style in War* (New York: Crane-Russak, 1982), pp. 367-383.
[26] Wohlstetter, "Bishops, Statesmen . . . ," *op. cit.*, pp. 25-26.

thinking. Neither Wohlstetter nor McNamara accept it as such today, yet it seems to me the only position that actually reconciles deterrence, reassurance, and defense, while at the same time being faithful to the moral imperative of desperately trying to maintain the normal without absolutely excluding the extreme.

It stands or falls, however, by what is always the ultimate political test: the ability to communicate moderation and resolve, the sense of responsibility which goes with freedom, and the feeling of awe before the destructive force waiting to be unleashed.

Morality, Arms Control, and Strategy

I have concentrated on nuclear and East-West issues, and particularly on the twin dangers of world destruction and totalitarian domination, because these are the issues raised by the European "peace movement" and symbolized by the "better red than dead" formula. But nuclear war is not the only danger facing mankind, nor is totalitarianism its only possible cause. While arms control may be less decisive than deterrence in preventing nuclear war, one specific goal which is clearly dictated by morality in a world of economic crisis and hunger is to strive for current levels of security at a lower cost and to redirect expenditures toward relieving poverty and spurring economic development in the Third World. Military expenditures grow more quickly in the Third World and lead more directly to actual wars, conventional and perhaps even someday nuclear, than the superpower arms race. It would thus seem that the imperatives of restraining nuclear proliferation and conventional arms sales and controlling Third World conflicts constitute a straightforward arms control agenda that is dictated by moral considerations.

And yet none of these issues offers an escape from the primacy of politics. The link between disarmament and development or the conversion from warfare to welfare is an inevitable feature for well-meaning speeches; taken globally, the comparison between the costs of submarines and hospitals, of keeping soldiers and feeding children, do point to a morally and intellectually revolting reality.

But nobody has been able to show how the reduction of one type of expenses could be made to benefit the other, short of a political reordering of domestic regimes and the international system. Similarly, the experiences of the nonproliferation treaty and the Carter Administration have shown the limits of universalistic and technological approaches to nonproliferation. The regional road, through alliances and guarantees, may offer more promise, but it may involve perpetuating the arms race (whose stabilization would be an incentive to proliferation) and going in the direction of

47

counterforce and missile defense. It certainly involves, at the least, more bilateral political bargaining than multilateral arms control.

Finally, the well-meaning attempts of the Carter Administration to reach agreements on limiting arms sales and on conventional arms control, particularly in areas like the Indian Ocean, have been wrecked by geostrategic asymmetries and political conflicts.[27] None of this means that the intentions of these policies were invalid or that the problems they addressed should be forgotten. But just as international politics cannot be reduced to military confrontation between East and West, so universalistic concerns with arms control and with economic redistribution cannot be abstracted from geostrategic and political asymmetries and conflicts. Kant said more or less that concepts without experience are empty, but experience without concepts is blind. We could conclude that in international affairs, morality and arms control are empty without a political strategy, but that without the guidance of the former, any political strategy is blind.

---

[27] See the sympathetic but pessimistic account, stressing the primacy of politics, by Barry Blechman, James Nolan, and Alan Platt, "Negotiated Limitations on Arms Transfers: First Steps Toward Crisis Prevention?," in Alexander L. George, editor, *Managing U.S.-Soviet Rivalry: Problems of Crisis Prevention* (Boulder, Col.: Westview Press, 1983), pp. 255-285.

Ethical Aspects of Nuclear Deterrence

by Laurence Martin

DETERRENCE as a purpose in the maintenance of armed forces and preparation for war is not new; it must always have been an element and often a conscious one in policy, as exemplified in the old adage "*si vis pacem*. . . ." It is not even novel to seek to deter by threatening not defeat but merely unacceptable losses to a would-be aggressor, as the naval doctrine of Tirpitz before the First World War and now the traditional armed neutralities of Sweden and Switzerland demonstrate. Nevertheless, modern-day nuclear deterrence is indeed different from that of preceding ages; it is differentiated both by the scale of consequences if it fails and by the fact that there is no obvious alternative in an effective strategy of defense.

The earliest theories of nuclear deterrence were indeed very much based on this absence of defense and the consequent necessity to seek security in the threat of retaliation. Both attack and retaliation were depicted almost entirely in terms of assaults on civilian society, or "city-busting." This image derived partly from the sheer scale of destruction made possible by the atomic bomb—so that it was not unnatural to assume targets would be large—and from the fact that throughout most of the Second World War, incompetence and inaccuracy on the part of bomber forces had precluded any effective long-range attacks on more precise objectives. While the resulting devastation of cities aroused disquiet among moralists, some justification was sought in the notion that, in a war of total mobilization, the whole enemy population was actively implicated in the war effort.

When the nuclear age began, therefore, the common model was of threat and riposte against cities with relatively little thought given to how such a war might have arisen or to what it would consequently take to deter it. It is true that the U.S. Air Force—and, so far as we know, Soviet strike forces—never wholly abandoned an interest in "military" or "war-potential" targets, a fact that is currently emphasized by some critics of the moralistic denunciation of nuclear deterrence. The fact remains, however, that for most of the nuclear era, the technology available did not permit much effective discrimination unless nuclear action was constrained to mere demonstrations. Even when military targets were envisaged, so-called collateral damage was frequently regarded as a bonus rather than a moral or practical problem.

Indeed, in declared policy, if not necessarily in actual targeting, American doctrine evolved under the name of assured destruction, to make civilian damage a virtue. Ironically, in view of his later pronouncements, this doctrine was never more explicitly enunciated than when Secretary of Defense Robert McNamara put numbers to the task of destroying the Soviet Union "as a twentieth century society."[1] Although this may have been partly an attempt to convince the armed services of the adequacy of U.S. strategic forces, it was the rhetoric of terror to which Winston Churchill had appealed much more robustly a decade earlier. The supposed virtue of a balance of terror, of mutual assured destruction, was to promote stability both in crisis and in the military balance, whereas strategies directed more discriminately at military targets entailed the prospect of open-ended competition matching one order of battle against another.

There are, however, numerous serious flaws in the concept of mutual assured destruction. Above all, it perpetuates the ever present possibility of mutual catastrophe; indeed, it depends precisely on this overhanging threat. The psychological strain of this relationship inevitably breeds efforts to escape by technological and strategic innovation—President Reagan's "Star Wars" proposals for defenses against missiles being a recent, if as yet rather implausible, example. Should the balance persist in a stable form, however, it opens up the possibility of neutralizing the nuclear weapon and thereby permitting the reappearance of large-scale conventional wars hitherto deterred between the nuclear powers by fear of escalation. But as the prospect of escalation can never be wholly discounted—even in a world of nuclear disarmament, rearmament is possible—the nuclear balance can in practice never be so stable as to preclude the realization of the otherwise stabilizing fear of holocaust. The complete elimination of the possibility of nuclear war would require a world devoid of political conflict. Moreover, the process of nuclear proliferation gradually increases the number of states between which these dangerous dilemmas exist.

Nuclear deterrence, then, including the simplistic form favored by the advocates of mutual assured destruction, carries in it the seeds of catastrophe. It does not follow, of course, that better policies necessarily exist, although a great many strategic and prudential issues could now be debated. The task here, however, is to discuss some of the moral implications.

Just War and Nuclear Weapons

There are clearly serious grounds for ethical concern. Any prospect of slaughter and destruction is ethically deplorable and the scale of devastation made possible by nuclear weapons all the more so. The blend of Christian and humanist thought in the West has sought to approach the problem of destructive war by evolving the doctrine of just war. While disclaim-

---

[1] The most explicit statement was in *The 1969 Defense Budget and Defense Program for Fiscal Years 1969-1973* (Washington, D.C.: Department of Defense, 22 January 1968), pp. 56 ff.

ing any pronounced capacity for interpreting that doctrine, it would seem to require that in deciding to go to war—the *jus ad bellum*—due proportion should be observed. But while it is never denied that some serious issue should be at stake, it has never been fully agreed whether there is a threshold of seriousness, which, once passed, justifies war pressed to a successful outcome, or whether the war effort itself should be continuously measured against the stakes.

In so far as proportionality should be observed during the war, we are brought close to the second aspect of the just war doctrine, the *jus in bello*, which requires a proportionality in the means used to relate the advantage of a tactic to its costs to enemy as well as friend. Moreover, a special value is placed on the welfare of noncombatants, to spare whom careful discrimination should be observed. War being justified to protect the innocent, it should not result in harming the innocent. In the words of Grotius, "nature does not sanction retaliation except against those who have done wrong. It is not sufficient that, by a sort of fiction, the enemy may be conceived of as forming a single body."[2] Since it is virtually impossible not to hurt some noncombatants, however, the principle of double-effect was evolved, which distinguishes between accidental injury to noncombatants and attacks launched specifically against them. For we must recognize that the doctrine of just war exists not to preclude war but to reconcile it to humanist and particularly Christian doctrine. Moreover, while the doctrine of just war may or may not be valid ethics, it has never been good history; that is to say, few wars have conformed to its strict interpretation.

If we try to relate the doctrine of just war to nuclear deterrence we should have little difficulty in agreeing that the actual execution of the nuclear strike tailored to assured destruction would fail the test. In its classic form such a strike is designed to kill civilians and destroy their property on the largest practicable scale. Even if the targeting emphasis were shifted from the population to the industrial and economic infrastructure—"recovery potential"—the collateral fatalities, the immediately consequent effects, and the longer term ecological results would grievously violate the duty of discrimination. Moreover, such an attack would very probably fail to satisfy the requirement of the *jus ad bellum* that there should be some realistic prospect of a successful outcome to the war, for in a state of mutual deterrence the concept of victory would be strained out of recognition.

This prospect of retaliation and mutual destruction naturally provides practical as well as moral reasons for hesitating to attack or press an attack to extremes. In other words, there are selfish as well as ethical reasons for observing proportionality founded on the desire to leave the enemy something to lose and therefore a reason to restrain his own attacks.

---

[2] *De Jura Belli et Pacis* (London: Carnegie edition, 1925), p. 741.

Nuclear Pacifism

These disturbing considerations have implications for the response of a would-be ethically responsible person. One is to adopt nuclear pacifism. This, it may be said, would entail potential surrender to any less scrupulous aggressor. In the words of the Bishop of London, "the worst weapons [would then be] solely in the worst hands" and entail that, "nuclear weapons, which the pacifist regarded as inherently evil, should be allowed to rest solely in the hands of those who had no scruple about their use, either in war or as blackmail."[3] To this the nuclear pacifist may reply that evil though such a condition may be, it pales into insignificance beside the consequences of nuclear war. Moreover, military conquest need not and perhaps rarely does mean moral or spiritual defeat and ultimately even political recovery may follow conquest. Cardinal Krol has maintained, for instance, that "the history of certain countries under Communist rule today shows that not only are human means of resistance available and effective but also that human life does not lose all meaning with replacement of one political system by another."[4] Such an outlook sometimes breeds an interest in the concept of "civilian resistance."

The contrary view was perhaps most sharply defined by Alexander Solzhenitsyn when he declared that it could not be better to be Red than dead because to be Red *was* to be dead. Christianity, it can be argued, does not require and indeed forbids surrender to evil, and the doctrine of just war was formulated precisely to avoid such a need. Nor has an individual wishing to sacrifice his freedom the right to impose such a sacrifice on his fellow citizens. A strategy entailing nuclear war also, of course, imposes an unpleasant fate on unwilling participants. Whether the fate of death is worse than that of lost freedom will be partly determined by one's idea of personal fulfillment. Early Christians looked forward with enthusiasm to Armageddon and the end of the world, but such a simple faith has not survived in many hearts.

The nuclear pacifist may, and if only perhaps for reasons of political argument often does, espouse conventional defense as an acceptable answer to the charge of passivity in the face of aggression. It seems rather doubtful, however, whether the dilemma can be escaped by this route. Modern conventional war on a large scale is a pretty unpleasant business itself, not devoid of many of the dilemmas raised by nuclear weapons. Conventional defense is also extremely expensive in men and money, and the demands of garrison states have consequences for the health of society to offset against the social tensions created by preservation of a nuclear balance. More to the

---

[3] Bishop Graham Leonard, General Synod, *Times* (London), February 11, 1983.
[4] In a sermon at the White House in 1979; quoted in *Commentary*, June 1983, p. 16.

immediate point, it is not clear why unilateral renunciation of nuclear weapons would not mean vulnerability to nuclear blackmail or defeat by nuclear weapons in war even if otherwise powerful conventional defenses had been maintained. To deny this requires a strong faith in the forebearance of a potential nuclear aggressor and in the current aura of "unthinkableness" about the use of nuclear weapons, bred in conditions of mutual deterrence, persisting into a less symmetrical balance. Given the ever present possibility of nuclear rearmament, now that the secret of the bomb is out, not even multilateral nuclear disarmament could guarantee the abolition of nuclear war; moreover, a world of conventional military preparations, and especially one actively engaged in conventional warfare, would be a fertile ground for such rearmament and transition to nuclear hostilities. Indeed, it is pretty clearly Western nuclear capabilities that have moved the Soviet Union to contemplate the possibility of war confined to conventional means. Nuclear disarmament would remove this deterrent. Thus, it seems questionable whether pacifism confined to nuclear weapons removes the objections to pacifism pure and simple, which seems, on its premises, the more coherent option.

It is theoretically and perhaps practically possible to modify nuclear pacifism even further and contemplate the possibility of warfare employing nuclear weapons only on a limited scale, thus attempting to preserve the deterrent effect of nuclear weapons while curbing their destructive effects. Very few people who devote much overt attention to the ethical aspects of nuclear warfare have much time for this speculation. Either they cannot imagine nuclear war on a less-than-catastrophic scale—a tendency enhanced by the rather large hypothetical nuclear engagements that are considered in the more widely read studies of supposedly limited nuclear war—or they rightly believe that the problems of escalation exist, if in different forms, in limited nuclear war. It is, indeed, important to note how central pessimism about the control of escalation is—a belief shared by many far from pacifist authorities, including the *"Foreign Affairs* Four," the former British Chief of Staff, Lord Carver, and the former U.S. Secretary of Defense, Harold Brown.[5] There would be widespread support for the syllogism that there are no degrees of nuclear war and that therefore all nuclear wars fail the tests of proportionality and discrimination.

The policy that the Western alliance upholds is not, of course, one of deliberately launching a major nuclear war as a first strike in an aggressive campaign but of responding to the initial aggressions of others. Does this

---

[5] The four are McGeorge Bundy, George Kennan, Robert McNamara, and Gerard Smith. See their article, "Nuclear Weapons and the Atlantic Alliance," *Foreign Affairs*, Spring 1982, pp. 753 ff; Lord Carver's views are in *A Policy for Peace* (London: Faber & Faber, 1982); Harold Brown's views are in several annual "posture" statements, e.g., *Department of Defense, Annual Report, Fiscal Year 1979* (Washington, D.C.: Department of Defense, 2 February 1978), p. 53; and the same title, *Fiscal Year 1980*, publication date 25 January 1979, pp. 75-76.

53

make any difference? The current doctrine of flexible response, in which nuclear weapons might be used first by NATO on a limited scale in response to conventional attacks that cannot otherwise be repelled, still falls foul of the belief in the indivisibility of nuclear war and the inevitability of escalation. Nevertheless, the intention of the Atlantic Alliance to go to nuclear war is conditional on prior aggression. The intention is not to have a nuclear war but to deter war altogether. The onus for the nuclear phase, it can be argued, falls on whoever was responsible for the war in the first place. Sherman is said to have declared in Georgia: "If the people raise a howl about my barbarity and cruelty, I will answer that war is war. . . . If they want peace they and their relatives must stop the war."[6]

Can we claim such justification for nuclear retaliation, whether in response to conventional or even nuclear aggression? Many would deny it. The consequences for the target population remain the same, and in many circumstances the execution of the retaliatory strike would indeed have no purpose other than revenge or the fulfillment of a theory for its own sake. Under certain circumstances it would be possible to reverse Sherman's argument and maintain that the aggressor would not have resorted to nuclear weapons if the defenders had not mounted a potential nuclear threat: this might be so, for instance, where the balance conferred a so-called first strike bonus.

One escape from condemnation of nuclear deterrence is to suggest that there is no need to execute the retaliation if deterrence fails. But this is a dubious recourse. If the deterrent is a patent bluff, it will not serve its purpose; to the extent that it is a somewhat but not wholly hollow sham, it may combine dangerous provocation with ineffectiveness. If, on the other hand, credibility is purchased by the maintenance of a genuine capability to retaliate and merely safeguarded by a secret intention not actually to do so, then, leaving aside the difficulty of preserving such a dire secret, there could be no certainty even in the minds of the architects of such a strategy that they could muster the necessary self-restraint *in extremis*, still less that they could bind their successors. Restraint might be forthcoming in the event, and some at least of the physical and moral consequences of nuclear war might be averted, but the ethical dilemmas inherent in a policy of deterrence would remain. Nor would the adversarial relationships engendered by postures of mutual nuclear threat be ameliorated.

The notion of enjoying the deterrent effect of nuclear weapons without really meaning it has come to infect the antinuclear movement itself. This hedging of bets is clearly visible in the recent report of a commission to the Church of England[7] and somewhat less so in the resolutions of the U.S. Catholic Bishops. In many other approaches to nuclear problems—in that

---

[6] Quoted in J.F.C. Fuller, *The Conduct of War, 1789-1961* (London: Methuen, 1972), p. 107.
[7] *The Church and the Bomb* (London: Hodder and Stoughton, 1982).

of the "*Foreign Affairs* Four" toward no first use, for example—the same hope of borrowing the deterrent aura from the policies being condemned and perpetuating them into the revised future can also be seen. At best, such hopes rest on a wasting asset; at worst, they may retain the provocative aspects of nuclear deterrence while eroding its stabilizing structures.

It is difficult to avoid the conclusion that if the supreme moral imperative is to preclude playing any active part in a nuclear war or being associated with the use of nuclear weapons, an imperative reinforced by the belief that any such use will lead in the end if not in the beginning to a major catastrophe, then the only satisfactory answer is nuclear pacifism and probably complete pacifism.

Peacekeeping, Restraint, and Deterrence

For some, however, this is not the end of the matter. Ethics is said to be a practical art—the art not of simply avoiding sinful acts, which in the real world frequently means martyrdom or impotence, but of minimizing evil in a world too imperfect to permit its complete exclusion. From this perspective the goal of avoiding implication in the use of nuclear weapons oneself may be less worthy than that of minimizing the probability that anyone at all will use them. In other words, in an imperfect world that is full of conflict and has discovered the secrets of the atom, it may be necessary to soil ourselves with nuclear strategy in an effort to save the world from nuclear war. Deterrence could be bad but right. Pacifism may be a luxury we should deny ourselves. As the new Archbishop of York wrote recently, with acknowledgment to the consistent theme of Reinhold Niebuhr: "One of the most disastrous mistakes Christians can make is to take absolutist elements in the Christian faith and translate them into programmes."[8]

If the supreme task is to prevent nuclear war, rather than to take no part in it if it occurs, then how to prevent it becomes a technical question of politics and strategy, though one naturally governed by ethical considerations, and still informed by the principles of proportionality and discrimination. The reasons for doubting whether policies of not possessing or threatening to use nuclear weapons might always be the best way to avert nuclear war, many of which were rehearsed earlier, now take on new significance. Pacifism may encourage blackmail and aggression; may send, in the recent words of the Archbishop of Canterbury, "misleading signals";[9] may destroy alliances which serve to restrain nuclear proliferation; may, in the inevitable time-consuming process of disarmament, even if mutual, project the strategic

---

[8] "Theological Reflections on Compromise," in N.A. Sims, editor, *Explorations in Ethics and International Relations* (London: Croom Helm, 1981), p. 115.
[9] At the General Synod, *Times* (London), February 11, 1983.

balance through highly unstable states—the last a good example of the need to measure superficially desirable processes against precise strategic and political criteria.

As a peacekeeping strategy, deterrence has many virtues. So long as it is successful, it is the least destructive strategy of all, perhaps the most subtle, proportionate and discriminating strategy available. It may, of course, fail, but so, as we have seen, may other approaches to the nuclear problem. If it does fail, must the consequence be assured destruction; must the prophets of inevitable escalation and catastrophe be vindicated? It would be foolhardy to deny that they may be; it is less clear that they must. The concept of limited nuclear war is currently in disfavor, suspected of making nuclear war more likely by raising hopes of control that would be dashed. In the 1930s the British strategic theorist J.F.C. Fuller looked back from the age of total war to the limited wars of the eighteenth century and declared them to be "a class of hot-house plant that can flourish in an aristocratic and qualitative civilisation. We are no longer capable of it."[10]

But in place of "civilization"—by no means an indisputable explanation even of the limitations that interested Fuller—we now have unprecedented fear as a motive for restraint. We have certainly demonstrated that we can still limit wars. The question is whether we can limit nuclear wars. This was a technical possibility the early theorists of nuclear deterrence did not enjoy, but technology has now provided the physical means of control and discrimination. The policy of mutual assured destruction virtually demands a lack of restraint and this has long colored all our images. But if limited nuclear war looks very bad compared to peace, it could look almost desirable when compared to the execution of assured destruction. Why should the first use of nuclear weapons lead to the immediate abandonment of restraint? Most such predictions are seen on examination to rest on the assumption of a Soviet refusal to moderate a response to a Western use of nuclear weapons. It naturally suits Soviet purposes to cultivate this impression in Western opinion, but it would scarcely be in the Soviet interest to confirm it in practice. There is a certain irony in the way that the sharpest critics of the Western policy of deterrence, who usually depict the United States as the least restrained party to the nuclear balance, should rest their denunciation of that policy on an assumption of Soviet recklessness.

The practicability of observing limitations on nuclear war is one of those complex and perhaps never wholly resolvable political and strategic questions requiring extensive discussion elsewhere. Here it is introduced only to suggest that deterrence, the ethics of which is the immediate problem, need not be identified solely with assured destruction. To peer beyond the veil of the collapse of deterrence and outbreak of nuclear war has its dangers,

---

[10] Fuller, *op. cit.*, p. 25.

but not to do so involves other hazards that would be bitterly regretted if the occasion arose. The essence of the charge against deterrence is, after all, its alleged indiscriminateness. To quote the Second Vatican Council: "Any act of war aimed indiscriminately at the destruction of entire cities or of extensive areas along with their population is a crime against God and man himself."[11] To inquire whether such indiscriminateness can be avoided seems consequently not merely legitimate but essential; the actual inquiry is a politico-strategic matter the answer to which must, of course, then be related to the ethical debate.

In pursuing that debate a perfectionist renunciation of nuclear deterrence should address some questions pertinent to an imperfect political world. Can any policy in a world privy to the secrets of the atom absolutely guarantee the prevention of nuclear war and, if not, are not all approaches to be compared on the same relative scale of practicability? Would deterrence be ethically condemned if political experts agreed it had virtual certainty of succeeding vis-à-vis an otherwise overwhelmingly powerful and universally detested aggressor? What if it was known that an aggressor would almost certainly use nuclear weapons to solve a strategic problem but would equally certainly be deterred by a countervailing nuclear threat? What if a few more years of deterrence provided a high probability of extensive disarmament? Why do so many pacifist exhortations include assurance that the Soviet Union is not aggressive? Would it make a difference if it were? Moreover, we must recognize that the Soviet Union is doubtless a passing phenomenon but nuclear energy will be with us forever.

Even if a policy of nuclear deterrence can be justified—or cannot be proved to be unjustifiable—it would still have to satisfy stern criteria. These would include the quality of the causes for which it is adopted and the skill with which it is executed. Such skill would embrace not merely political and strategic competence but also attention to technical safety and security of custody, immensely responsible tasks all too rarely addressed in the wider debate. To discharge these tasks is neither easy nor cheap, and it is a further cause for uneasiness about the renunciationists that their influence rarely supports in practice—though for tactical reasons their rhetoric sometimes does—the provision of material resources to alleviate the dangers of the nuclear balance, whether by way of intrinsic improvements or conventional alternatives.

Finally, it must be emphasized that, even if nuclear deterrence can be justified, it should not be overburdened. Even if effective limitations for nuclear war were devised, it should not be regarded as a scaled-down, mini-version of massive retaliation. Deterrence is a continuum stretching not

---

[11] "Gaudium et Spes," Article 80, in the translation of W.M. Abbott, *The Documents of Vatican II* (London: Geoffrey Chapman, 1966).

merely into the realms of conventional defense but also to diplomacy and conciliation. Endemic conflict may be an inevitable feature of international society, but we have a duty to mitigate it even at considerable cost to ourselves. Freed of the special connotations of the 1930s, the notion of appeasement deserves rehabilitation. Moreover, appeasement has its place even in nuclear strategy if we strive responsibly to avoid needlessly provocative or destabilizing postures. The most responsible form of unilateralism is, indeed, a constant and voluntary attention to the contribution of our own military and especially nuclear policies to global safety. This requires not revulsion from the mechanisms of deterrence but a constant and ethically informed attention to them.

The Moral Implications of Strategic Deterrence

by Michael Novak

At one time there was no comparison between the strength of the USSR and yours. Then it became equal. . . . Perhaps today it is just greater than balance, but soon it will be two to one. Then three to one. Finally it will be five to one. . . . With such a nuclear superiority it will be possible to block the use of your weapons, and on some unlucky morning they will declare: "Attention. We're marching our troops to Europe, and if you make a move, we will annihilate you." And this ratio of three to one, of five to one, will have its effect: you will not make a move.[1]
Aleksandr Solzhenitsyn

D URING THE LAST ten years, there has been a great change in Western public opinion concerning nuclear weapons—and also a great change in reality. The change in reality is fundamental. At the time of the first SALT accords in 1972, it was agreed that the Soviet Union through prodigious efforts since the Cuban missile crisis of 1962 had achieved "essential parity" with the United States. From 1972 to 1980, three fundamental changes occurred: (1) Soviet strategic nuclear forces grew at rates unmatched by the United States; (2) Soviet *conventional* arms achieved virtual parity in quality with NATO conventional arms, while maintaining huge advantages in quantity; and (3) in 1977, the Soviets began placing Western Europe within targeting range of a ring of powerful new, highly accurate SS-20s, against which the West had no appropriate deterrent.

Fear of Nuclear Conflict

These fundamental changes in the balance of power in Europe—strategic nuclear, conventional, and theater nuclear—induced considerable fear. This fear is entirely appropriate. What is done with this fear is one of the greatest moral questions of our time.

This fear is entirely appropriate, because the nuclear initiative has, for the time being, passed to the Soviets. They have acted first and successfully. More profoundly, they now have a wider range of nuclear choices—and

---

[1] Quoted in Robert Jastrow, "Why Strategic Superiority Matters," *Commentary*, March 1983, p. 32.

less constraint of every sort upon those choices—than NATO does. Andrei Sakharov addresses this point with some alarm:

Precisely because an all-out nuclear war means collective suicide, we can imagine that a potential aggressor might count on a lack of resolve on the part of the country under attack to take the step leading to that suicide, i.e., it could count on its victim capitulating for the sake of saving what could be saved. Given that, if the aggressor has a military advantage in some of the variants of conventional warfare or—which is also possible *in principle*—in some of the variants of partial (limited) nuclear war, he would attempt to use the fear of further escalation to force the enemy to fight the war on his (the aggressor's) own terms. . . . Now take the next logical step—while nuclear weapons exist it is also necessary to have strategic parity in relation to those variants of limited or regional nuclear warfare which a potential enemy could impose, i.e., it is really *necessary* to examine in detail the various scenarios for both conventional and nuclear war and to analyze the various contingencies. It is of course not possible to analyze fully all these possibilities or to ensure security entirely. But I am attempting to warn of the opposite extreme—"closing one's eyes" and relying on one's potential enemy to be perfectly sensible.[2]

My colleague, Irving Kristol, the distinguished editor of *The Public Interest*, holds that the nuclear umbrella which once protected Europe has now collapsed. It is no longer credible that U.S. strategic nuclear weapons can deter an attack by Soviet conventional forces upon Europe; nor can they deter a nuclear attack by the Soviets on some part of Europe. For why would the United States commit nuclear suicide? He argues further that the remaining 300,000 U.S. soldiers stationed in Europe no longer serve a useful purpose. On the contrary, he asserts, as hostages they expose the United States to nuclear blackmail, and they prevent the Europeans from becoming realistic about their own defense. He believes that reality will soon oblige the United States to withdraw its forces from Europe.

This is an extreme view. But its logic, however much cold fear it induces, is compelling.

In short, the Soviet SS-20s have already become one of the most successful weapons systems in the history of Europe; without ever being fired, they have shaken the ground. A kind of terror is in the air.

Perceptions of the Soviet Union

It is a first moral obligation to still fear with the cool light of reason. Reason should never yield to terror. Moreover, the lessons of 1938 are clear. Appeasement does not avert war; sometimes it makes war both inevitable and more terrible than if determined resistance had been shown at earlier stages.

Much has been written about differences in perception concerning the Soviet Union. In recent debates, four different perceptions among West

---

[2] Andrei Sakharov, "The Danger of Thermonuclear War," *Foreign Affairs*, Summer 1983, p. 1010.

Europeans have emerged. First, the Soviet Union and the United States are relatively *equal* threats to European safety and security; they are, in some ways, mirror images. European neutralism is the way to peace. Second, the Soviet Union is not so much an aggressive, expansionist power as it is a victim of historical paranoia, justified in part by current feelings of being surrounded by Western powers. Third, leaders in the United States, particularly in the Reagan Administration, overestimate "the Soviet threat," and thus lack the more balanced, nuanced view of Europeans who live closer to the USSR. Fourth, Soviet power is awesome and dangerous—a view shared by most Europeans and Americans—but there are many differences of judgment about appropriate responses, both among Europeans and between Europe and America.

Without getting into a debate here about the nature and destiny of Soviet power, I want only to make a crucial distinction between *intentions, proclivities,* and *strategic potential*. It seems to be a wise principle in charting any program of defense—whether in chess, in soccer, in commerce, or in military-strategic thinking—to keep in mind a "worst case" view of the array of possibilities open to an opponent. Failure to do so invites terrible surprises, encourages complacency, and nourishes illusions.

Thus, in the first place, one needs a clearheaded analysis of the range of options open to the opponent, given his strategic assets. These represent the opponent's *strategic potential*. The factors involved include not only the technical capabilities of his assets, but also his command and control capacities and strategic doctrines. It is important to emphasize that strategic potential consists of much more than merely material assets.

Second, one needs to analyze carefully the *proclivities* of an opponent. Of these, the relevant components are in one sense more elusive, and yet in another sense far better known. For these include factors of history and culture, institutions and the character of leadership, and habits of mind and thought, encompassing not only formal ideology but also (and even more importantly) well-established patterns and habits of behavior. It was in this sense, for example, that the American Founding Father James Madison said that the Constitution of the United States has its real existence not in the "parchment barrier" of a few words on paper, but in the character and the institutions of the American people. In analyzing the proclivities of the Soviet Union, clear thought requires attention to the continuing power of Russian culture, to the tradition of old-fashioned Russian geopolitical ambition, to the actual weight of the Marxist-Leninist sense of historical destiny, and to the bureaucratic imperatives of the Soviet ruling elite. From such factors flow the spiritual component, the will, which actualizes strategic potential.

Third, one needs to estimate (since certain knowledge is not possible) the *intentions* of the current leadership. Much more attention is usually given to intentions than to proclivities. This is a mistake, because a grasp of intentions is inherently based upon a high degree of guesswork, whereas proclivities are far more stable, more knowable, and more closely related to real interests. In addition, the Leninist doctrine of the "correlation of forces" instructs Soviet leaders clearly enough to keep a cool judgment about the probabilities of success and failure. Such judgment tilts Soviet analysis away from evanescent intentions and toward more secure and established proclivities. To be sure, totalitarian leadership is inherently vulnerable to naked seizures of will—*la feroce volontà* as Mussolini called it, and as Stalin exercised it. But "collective leadership" of the Soviet style and Marxist-Leninist doctrine mitigate this tendency.

All three factors are important. Moral analysis suggests that strategic potential and proclivities are the most decisive.

Crisis of the Spirit in the West

These points have been raised at the beginning because the very first requirement of "just war" thinking requires an exact analysis of "the just cause." If the Soviet Union were constituted as a nation like other nations, our task today would be far simpler than it is. For when we in the West speak of "deterrence," we have in mind almost exclusively the deterrence of the Soviet Union. Our own democracies do not threaten one another. This is not only because we together form an alliance but, rather, because we each value self-determination, mutual collaboration in the pursuit of peaceful commerce and cultural interchange, and the beneficent (although difficult) rule of liberty and law. All our concentrated energy of deterrence crystallizes around only one threat: that of the Soviet Union.

Here, indeed, Europeans may be by tradition better analysts of the Soviet Union than we—so far away—in the United States. Nevertheless, Europeans, especially younger ones, face special spiritual temptations which may blunt inherent European advantages. Having experienced two world wars on their soil in almost successive generations in this century, Europeans must view a third Continental conflict, in a poignant way, as unthinkable. Furthermore, from 1945 until the present—for almost forty years—a broken, and then a prosperous, Europe has counted on the U.S. nuclear umbrella to keep war away. There must be immense disappointment in Europe, however irrational such a feeling might seem in the court of cold reason, that the nuclear umbrella has been pierced—as if the Americans should somehow have prevented it. There seems to be considerable anger at Americans among at least some small (but visible) parts of the population, and this anger seems coincident with the emergence of the three new strategic realities I mentioned at the outset: the tangible growth of Soviet strategic, conventional, and theater nuclear power during the last six years.

It is neither just nor useful to blame Europeans for the sudden emergence of fear and misdirected anger, the underlying cause of which is actually a moral crisis. For societies which are simultaneously democratic, capitalist (or social market), and pluralistic carry within them two virtues which are also defects. First, productive of unprecedented prosperity and liberty (and which generation of European youths ever lived in greater personal abundance and liberty?), such societies soon erode the martial virtues. Based upon relations which are pacific, law-abiding, commercial, and libertarian, such societies almost by deliberation discourage the taste for physical bravado, for martial glory, and even for the heroic. Instead, they instill a due regard for small gains and losses, for prudence and mutual regard, for practical accomplishment, and for a spirit of mutual adjustment and compromise. This is not the stuff of heroism. Peace itself is an unheroic sort of life, given to smoothing troubled waters and concentrating attention on the calm resolution, rather than on the dramatic escalation, of passional conflict. In short, the democratic, commercial, pluralist spirit is quite different from the spirit of the knights, the feudal warlords, and the martial talents which so distinguished the leadership of European civilization only a few generations ago. As Ralph Lerner observes:

The old order was preoccupied with intangible goods to an extent we now hardly ever see. The king had his glory, the nobles their honor, the Christians their salvation, the citizens of pagan antiquity their ambition to outdo others in serving the public good. . . . The weightier truth, however, was that concern with these fancies skewed public policy and public budgets, sacrificing the real needs of the people to the petty desires of their governors.[3]

It is not easy to arouse democratic peoples to thoughts of wars, crusades, and noble military causes. People in the mass (those we used to call the common people), expressing themselves through self-government, seldom share the extreme spirituality of the clergy, the aristocrat's natural longing for glory, or the military's proper longing to demonstrate courage and competence in combat.

The second part of the crisis of the spirit flows from the same source. In order to function effectively, a society which is democratic, commercial, and pluralistic must quite deliberately avoid intense *official* concentration upon moral, spiritual, and religious matters. Pluralism and liberty of conscience exact this price. For in the depths of the human spirit, each person has an autonomy and personal responsibility which no official power can either take away or fully express. Public authorities, therefore, and not only those of the state, but also those of the universities, the media, and others,

---

[3] Ralph Lerner, "Commerce and Character: The Anglo-American as New-Model Man," *William and Mary Quarterly*, January 1979, p. 5; reprinted in Michael Novak, editor, *Liberation South, Liberation North* (Washington, D.C.: American Enterprise Institute, 1981).

are obliged to maintain an historically unprecedented taciturnity. In the religious states of the past, in homogeneous states, public figures not only voiced the profound communal convictions of all, they *represented* them in their persons. When Charlemagne knelt to be crowned by the Pope—as Napoleon wished to be two centuries ago—all Europe, in a sense, knelt with him. Such homogeneity of spirit is no longer thought to be appropriate to a people free and pluralistic in spirit, not precisely because the state is secular but because the state is pluralistic. A sort of spiritual abnegation is required in public, a refusal to exercise an *imperium* over conscience. This is, I think, a noble self-abnegation. But it exacts high costs.

One of those costs is that public figures—and again I insist that journalists, artists, professors, and many others bear the same costs as those borne by public officials—no longer effectively speak, in the full sense, as moral, spiritual, or religious authorities for all. This fact means that modern societies like those which compose NATO may at first appear to the nostalgic eye as being spiritually empty. One phrase some religious writers use for this phenomenon is "practical atheism" or "practical materialism"—that is, not atheism or materialism in *principle*, but silence or emptiness or (more exactly) spiritual chastity, exactly where in earlier eras, not so long ago, there was public satisfaction.

Is it any wonder, then, that the immature observer, looking over our public life, should declare that Western Europe and the United States seem to be, as far as the eye sees or the ear hears, as spiritually empty as Eastern Europe, though rather in practice than in principle? This is an immature and dangerous way of thinking. But it is surely common enough.

These are the two chief reasons why Western nations seem, at first glance, to be losing the battle of the human spirit. It is not easy for Western men and women in public roles to voice their own most profound human convictions, their moral principles, the secrets of their own spiritual lives. Simple due regard for the analogous but quite different spiritual autobiographies of their colleagues and fellow citizens prevents them from seeming to demand full consent for what they themselves deem most important in human life, the springs of their own spiritual journey. To infer from this decent silence, this profound regard for others, a "spiritual emptiness" is a great error. In public, there *is* a spiritual emptiness, but out of self-abnegation and a respect for the proper liberties of the human soul of each. This system denies itself what earlier types of social systems did not deny themselves. This is not a fault, but a high and precious virtue. Yet it is also, in public affairs, a serious weakness.

For human beings are, above all, symbolic animals. They hunger for publicly, communally acclaimed values. One sees this vividly in the young. The virtues of societies which are democratic, capitalist, and pluralistic are not easily learned by the young. These are, after all, the virtues acquired

64

through the lessons of experience: realism, moderation, prudence, a spirit of compromise, and "loyal opposition" (in which one agrees, in civility, to disagree and to abide by consensual methods). These might be said to be the virtues of middle age, chary of the romantic sense of the young and not yet accustomed to the detached wisdom of the aged. Literature speaks well of the young and of the old. Religion, too, finds more direct access to the young and to the old. Middle age, less sung in song, is the age of activism in political economy.

When we come, then, to articulate our middle-aged reasons for our highest ideals, and for their defense against hostile forces, we find ourselves acting against our accustomed grain. Bishops easily enough speak of moral principles and high visions, and for that we may be grateful. Yet the task of those whose vocation calls them to make political economies work, and in particular adequately to defend themselves, demands far greater uncertainties, awareness of improbable contingencies, and an instinct for how difficult is the execution of any alternative whatever.

We all wish that the threats which now face our civilization did not exist. We wish we did not have to face them. As President Kennedy once said, "Life is unfair." He also spoke, in his Inaugural Address, of our generation's "call to bear the burden of a long twilight struggle, year in and year out," and he continued: "In the long history of the world, only a few generations have been granted the role of defending freedom in its hour of maximum danger. I do not shrink from this responsibility—I welcome it. I do not believe that any of us would exchange places with any other generation."[4] So is our struggle, still today, for moral clarity in a nuclear age.

Our cause is just, for the existence of our liberties is at risk. The disguised threat is that of living under intimidation, obliged to do what we would choose not to do, by some degree living under a regime to which we do not give free assent.

Nuclear Weapons: Possession and Intention

Nuclear weapons have four functions. The first is to yield a sense of sovereignty and prestige; thus, France and Britain have borne heavy expense to maintain an independent deterrent force, and the USSR has reasons beyond those of defense for its efforts to rank as the greatest of the "superpowers." The second is for intimidation, since nuclear arsenals speak louder than words and evoke in less well-armed neighbors both awe and respect. The third is for deterrence; thus, the "nuclear umbrella" of the United States was once judged to be the most moral, least burdensome, and most effec-

---

[4] Press conference of March 21, 1962, in *Public Papers of the Presidents of the United States: John F. Kennedy, 1961*, 3 volumes (Washington, D.C.: U.S. Government Printing Office, 1963), Vol. 2, p. 259; and Inaugural Address, *ibid.*, Vol. 1, pp. 1-2.

tive method of containing Soviet ambitions with respect to Europe and Japan. The fourth is the function most popularly recognized, that of an actual instrument of war. It is important to recognize that the first three functions, whatever their individual merits, do not require the actual use of nuclear weapons. The most popularly recognized and justly feared function of nuclear weapons, the last, is but one of four actual functions.

In an earlier paper, published both in America and in Germany, I asserted that a chief moral imperative of our age is to prevent both the unjust military use of nuclear weapons in actual war and the unjust use of such weapons for purposes of intimidation.[5] I also observed, with the Second Vatican Council of the Roman Catholic Church, that the existence of new scientific weapons obliges moralists to think about war "in a way entirely new." In practice, not everything about the morality of nuclear weapons is "entirely new." But one thing that is new concerns the intention proper to deterrence.

Some moralists seek to wash their hands of moral responsibility by saying that it is permissible to *possess* nuclear weapons, but wrong in any way to *use* them or to *intend* to use them in military combat. This is casuistry of the worst sort. It is based on moral approval of the function of deterrence, but it then falls into two fallacies. The first fallacy is that the mere possession of nuclear weapons will deter an aggressor, since the aggressor will not "believe" that the weapons will remain unused. But this is to suppose that an aggressor will refrain from provocations, probes, and tests of will. This is an exceedingly dangerous supposition. The true intention of this so-called moral position is that of Pilate; to wish to pretend to moral responsibility by indulging in hypocrisy.

The second fallacy is to suppose that the *possession* of a nuclear deterrent does not itself include *intentions*. In a free society, citizens must vote the funds; parliamentarians must allocate them; military strategists must design the deterrent; companies must build its material components; officers and men must be trained to keep it in readiness. A deterrent is not inert metal; it is an intentional process, which must be held always at the ready. "Intentions" are not solely internal subjective acts; they are also organizing principles of activity. The young enlisted man of eighteen who boards a Trident submarine as it leaves for its duty station is engaged in *intentional* activity, whatever his subjective state of mind.

Thus, it is simply not possible to possess a deterrent *without exercising its inherent intentionality*. The concept of a deterrent necessarily includes both an internal organizing principle (an intention in that sense) and an implied threat to the one who is being deterred (an intention in that further

---

[5] "Moral Clarity in the Nuclear Age," *Catholicism in Crisis*, March 1983; published also in *National Review*, April 1, 1983. In German, see *Argumente für Frieden und Freiheit*, Research Report 25 of the Konrad-Adenauer-Stiftung (Melle: Ernst Knoth, 1983), pp. 13-24.

sense). The concept of a deterrent which has no intention and makes no threat is empty. No one could be led to such a concept except through moral evasion.

Next, we must note that the concept of intention must be applied differently in the following cases: (1) a direct premeditated, unconditioned action; and (2) an action of deterrence. To intend to *do* something and to intend to *prevent* something are two different types of action. Furthermore, the act of deterrence typically embodies a threat, although of a peculiar sort. A parent often tells a child, "I'll tan your hide!," or voices a similar fearsome threat. Policemen carry threatening equipment. Embassies are guarded. Crowd control even at a peaceful concert often involves mounted police or police with dogs. Deterrence is necessary in ordinary, peaceful human life because human behavior is not always rational. One would wish (even God would wish) that human beings loved God freely and willingly obeyed his law; the fires of Gehenna are invoked as an additional deterrent.

Indeed, even the peace movement depends indispensably upon the deterrent value of images of mass destruction. Without this threat, the movement would lack passion.

The peculiar structure of intention in deterrence deserves clarification. It is true that if in premeditated resolution an assassin sets out to murder the Pope, but fails, then he has "already committed murder in his heart," and *morally speaking* (even legally speaking) is as guilty in the attempt as in its success. But the case of those who intend to deter such an act is quite different. If one's premeditated resolution is to *deter* an assassin, then the intention is fulfilled if and only if the deterrence works—if a potential assassin is kept out of reach, is discouraged, or is detected and disarmed. Should one actually have to *use* one's deterrent weapons, a *breakdown* in deterrence has occurred. At this point, deterrence is no longer the operating activity from a moral point of view; one must shift to the logic of direct action.

With respect to the nuclear deterrent, it must be obvious that its fundamental intention is to deter unjust aggressive actions by another. "To do good and to avoid evil" is the fundamental moral law, under which such a fundamental intention clearly falls. A complication arises because inherent in the organizing principle of deterrence is an intention of conditional use; an effective deterrent tells a potential aggressor: "Avoid evil acts lest you be punished by my deterrent force." The will to inflict punishment is inherent in the deterrent. Without such will, the "deterrent" becomes only a symbol of law and reason, perhaps like the ceremonial pikestaffs of the Swiss Guards in the Vatican. Ceremonial deterrents are not designed to deter a determined aggressor, only one already committed to justice and to law.

Morality and the Nuclear Deterrent

At this point, some question the moral validity of the nuclear deterrent, not insofar as it is a deterrent, but insofar as it requires a will to punish the aggressor in case deterrence fails. This formulation, however, shows that their moral objection does not aim directly at deterrence, whose moral legitimacy it concedes. It aims, rather, at the *breakdown* of deterrence. Yet if we ask what might cause deterrence to break down or, conversely, how we might best contrive to make certain that it does not break down, we see immediately that the greatest moral danger lies in an inadequate deterrent. The logic of nuclear deterrence is to prevent certain forms of unjust aggression and further to prevent any use of nuclear weapons whatever. Only in the fulfillment of these two goals does deterrence fulfill its mission. This mission is moral. Indeed, the sacrifices and discipline required to maintain its vigilance require high moral courage and nobility of soul.

Those responsible for the breakdown of deterrence, therefore, bear a tragic moral responsibility. Even the attempt to acquire deterrence "on the cheap" seems, in this light, morally reprehensible. For doubts about the adequacy of deterrence positively solicit bold and aggressive probes. Thus, doubts about Western resolve clearly underlie the bold Soviet program of building an Iron Ring of SS-20s just behind the Iron Curtain. Given Soviet *proclivities* to advance wherever weakness is apparent, the attempt by Western powers to buy deterrence "on the cheap" during the 1970s illustrates the moral peril into which illusions quickly plunge the morally weak.

A plausible rejoinder to this line of argument is that it seems to lead inexorably to "an arms race," with each side expending ever new resources to keep deterrence credible. Three points need here to be observed. First, sheer material obsolescence requires fresh generational expenses simply to replace old equipment. (The generational retirement of obsolescent systems which have never been used in war is the clearest possible evidence that deterrence works.)

Second, despite popular perceptions to the contrary, spending on conventional arms is far more expensive, by a factor of at least nine-to-one, than spending on the nuclear deterrent. In the United States, military spending in constant 1983 dollars dropped 19 percent between 1970 and 1981, from $223.1 to $181.5 billion. Throughout that period spending on nuclear weapons constituted only 8 percent of all military spending.[6]

Third, the generational replacement of the nuclear deterrent—a process which typically requires fifteen years—affords each new generation of leaders an opportunity to think anew about *moral improvements* in the nature

---

[6] Testimony of Hon. David A. Stockman, Director, Office of Management and Budget, before the Joint Economic Committee, U.S. Congress, May 4, 1983. Nuclear weapons expenditures are computed from the National Defense Budget Estimates published annually by the Office of the Assistant Secretary of Defense (Comptroller).

of weapons systems.[7] In the first generation, for example, from about 1945 to 1960, the *moral character* of the deterrent force was at its crudest. During this period, the United States had a virtual nuclear monopoly. Its first generation of warheads was characterized by very large megatonnage and only marginal accuracy, so that their main threat was to Soviet urban centers. This was the least moral system.

The second generation of U.S. systems, put in place in the 1960s, was composed of much smaller warheads and more accurate guidance systems. As the Soviet systems grew in size, this period was at first characterized by the relatively simple but still crude doctrine of Mutual Assured Destruction. Each side targeted each other's cities. But a more sophisticated and, from a moral point of view, much superior strategy of deterrence began to evolve: Flexible Response. This strategy permitted the targeting of military targets in addition to, or rather than, urban populations.

Finally, in the third stage of development, beginning about 1975, advances in technology permitted the construction of smaller warheads and guidance systems of far greater accuracy. Clear advances were made in the direction of *proportionality* and *discrimination*. So great were these advances, indeed, that some moralists began to worry that nuclear strategy might be becoming too "reasonable," by beginning to fall into the classical moral logic that governs large conventional weapons. They began to fear that the smaller nuclear weapons were beginning to resemble (in proportionality and discrimination) the larger conventional weapons. They applauded this development for its superior moral structure. But they also began to fear that the psychological barrier between conventional warfare and nuclear warfare was beginning to weaken. Moreover, the continuing existence of large warheads and vastly increased throwweight (especially on the Soviet side) afforded an ominous backdrop to the newer, smaller, and more accurate weapons. Some moralists, therefore, fell into moral conflict in their own minds, torn between approval of weaponry more proportional and discriminating, on the one hand, and fears about lowering the threshold of horror which accrues to *all* nuclear weapons, on the other.[8]

During these last three systemic generations, deterrence has been based upon *offensive* weapons rather than upon *defensive* weapons. This fact presents a moral challenge for our own generation. The *moral superiority* of defensive weapons is obvious. For the right to self-defense—and for states, the *duty* of self-defense—is much more neatly underlined by defensive than by of-

---

[7] See Albert Wohlstetter, "Bishops, Statesmen and Other Strategists on the Bombing of Innocents," *Commentary*, June 1983, pp. 15-35.

[8] J. Bryan Hehir, for example, contends that "counterforce strategy is subject to the criticism that it makes nuclear war "thinkable," increasing the probability of wars being started with such weapons or of such weapons being employed because they are controllable, with one side or both tempted to escalate the conflict to an 'all-out' nuclear exchange." "The Catholic Church and the Arms Race," *Worldview*, July-August 1978, p. 15.

fensive deterrents. Furthermore, in the interests of mutual stability, nations intent solely upon self-defense may quite reasonably *share* the technology of defensive systems with their foes. President Reagan, accordingly, has made just this offer to the Soviets, looking ahead to the strategy of deterrence a generation from now. Second, a defensive shield is much more clearly a "nuclear umbrella" than is an offensive deterrent. Indeed, it is intellectually conceivable—and perhaps technically feasible, a judgment not for the moralist but for scientists to assess—that current arsenals of intercontinental ballistic missiles might one day be rendered obsolete. For if it were possible accurately to detect and swiftly to destroy offensive weapons shortly after their blast-off, such weapons would become a threat not to their intended targets but to those who launched them.

Admittedly, we now enter the realm of speculation about future possibilities. But this very fact is evidence of sound moral thinking. For moral thinking is, first of all, thinking about possible better futures, about ends and purposes, about creative advances. The human race is not condemned forever to immobility and resignation to the present. Human intellect and will are free.

Consider the alternatives advanced by rival futurists. Jonathan Schell in *The Fate of the Earth* imagines that the future solution to present dilemmas lies in a benign, tolerant, peaceful, rational "world government."[9] The Catholic Bishops of the United States even propose the model of the United Nations as a harbinger of such a development![10] Yet the minute one tries to imagine the conversion of the Soviet Union to the ideals of such a vision of world government, one sees the absurdity of the wish. The solution proposed is merely a wishing away of the problem to be met. For the sole problem arises from the nature of the Soviet Union. Against no other nation is nuclear deterrence necessary. Those who argue that the government of the United States is also a potential threat cannot, logically, have faith in the moral quality of *world* government, if civil democratic government cannot even guarantee moral confidence in the United States.

Still others react to present perplexities by urging a "nuclear freeze." Yet it is difficult to see how this is anything but a counsel of despair. For a "freeze"

---

[9] "We must lay down our arms, relinquish sovereignty, and found a political system for the peaceful settlement of international disputes. . . . Since the goal would be a nonviolent world, the actions of this endeavor would be nonviolent. . . . With the world itself at stake, all differences would by definition be 'internal' differences, to be resolved on the basis of respect for those with whom one disagreed." Jonathan Schell, *The Fate of the Earth* (New York: Avon Books, 1982), pp. 226, 229. See also Walter Berns, "The New Pacifism and World Government," *National Review*, May 27, 1983, pp. 613-620.

[10] The bishops' pastoral letter states: "Just as the nation-state was a step in the evolution of government at a time when expanding trade and new weapons technologies made the feudal system inadequate to manage conflicts and provide security, so we are now entering an era of new, global interdependencies requiring global systems of governance to manage the resulting conflicts and ensure our common security. . . . As we shall indicate below, the United Nations should be particularly considered in this effort." "The Challenge of Peace: God's Promise and Our Response," *Origins*, May 19, 1983, p. 23.

does nothing to remove current inadequacies in deterrence. Quite the contrary. It locks in place exactly those sorts of imbalances which have generated the current wave of fear. Its true message is not, as it says, that the arms race is "blind" but that, just as blindly, human beings can do nothing but say "halt." Under the lash of fear, the freezing of the human capacity to think and to act is understandable, but it is hardly admirable and not in the least hopeful. Moreover, the hidden condition for a successful nuclear freeze lies in its demand upon the USSR to permit the on-site verification not only of nuclear weapons deployed (many of them undetectable by satellite technology) but also of easily disguised research and development. This condition requires a hopefulness about Soviet proclivities which is contradicted by history. It must also be counted as a wishing away of the fundamental problem.

Finally, there are some—see, for example, certain passages in the U.S. Bishops' Pastoral Letter—who are already imagining preemptive surrender. Contemplating Eastern Europe, some are already saying that they would willingly live under such a regime, addressing against it "civilian resistance" and "passive resistance" in the confident hope that after two or three generations they would "convert" it from within. Their confidence in their own virtue—which, of course, they attribute to their faith in God—is quite touching. Do they imagine themselves as future Orlovs, Sakharovs, and Solzhenitsyns? Since they are already willing to renounce their moral obligation to defend the innocent from unjust aggression, one wonders what next moral renunciation they will make. Perhaps they think that "liberation theology" will enable them to subvert Marxism-Leninism through Christian Marxism. They do not seem to glimpse the contempt in which they will properly be held by their new masters, who will judge that their unwillingness to fight for the institutions of liberty constitutes a preemptive devaluation of such institutions. This devaluation is already quite congenial to those whom they aim to "convert."

It will be noted that all of these alternatives—world government, a nuclear freeze, and preemptive surrender—share a common theme. Each is naive about political institutions. Each has in mind the freedom of the moral individual, *as if this freedom were not constituted by specific institutions of civil and political liberties*: parliaments, opposition parties, courts, a free press, private property, a limited state, and the like. Thus, "world government" implies that all the world shares the habits, values, and institutional forms of civil discourse and the consent of the governed. The nuclear freeze depends upon the Soviet Union becoming an open society.[11] Preemptive surrender rests

---

[11] Andrei Sakharov observes: "I know that pacifist sentiments are very strong in the West. I deeply sympathize with people's yearning for peace, for a solution to world problems by peaceful means; I share those aspirations fully. But, at the same time, I am certain that it is absolutely necessary to be mindful of the specific political, military, and strategic realities of the present day and to do

upon a thoroughly spiritual and nonpolitical vision of Christianity and civilization. In short, in the name of "preserving the values of the West," each overlooks the *nature* of Western achievements. For these achievements lie precisely in the development of specific kinds of political and economic *institutions*, built up through the centuries of moral thinking, political struggle, and no little bloodshed. All this is now to be counted as nothing, in the light of "higher" spiritual values. In the place of humble, imperfect but manifestly functioning institutions, we are instructed to trust the spiritual life of individuals.

The West has already had many historical battles with the Gnostics, the Cathars, and Spiritualists of every sort. What the West has learned from such struggles is the self-abnegation required to build humble institutions which promise utopias to none but liberty and due regard for individual rights to all. The "values" of the West most now to be defended are not so much "spiritual" as "political"—incarnated in specific institutions. Those who love these institutions, and who intend to defend them with their lives, their fortunes, and their sacred honor, are *not* defending "spiritual values" in the abstract, but rather those *institutions* which permit individuals, alone or in association, to follow truth, conscience, and love wherever these may lead. It is concrete institutions which are the objects of our loyalty and our devotion. It is these which we defend against all enemies. It is around these institutions, through them, and by their empowering our diverse consciences that we intend to deter every threat from every enemy, in whatever form it may come.

In this respect, our purposeful public silence about the spiritual values that diversely move each of us is not a weakness. We love, and we will defend, the *institutions* which permit to us such respectful public silence, for only such institutions, history has taught us, truly liberate the human soul.

---

so objectively without making any sort of allowances for either side; this also means that one should not proceed from an *a priori* assumption of any special peace-loving nature in the socialist countries due to their supposed progressiveness or the horrors and losses they have experienced in war. Objective reality is much more complicated and far from anything so simple. People both in the socialist and the Western countries have a passionate inward aspiration for peace. This is an extremely important factor, but, I repeat, itself alone does not exclude the possibility of a tragic outcome." Sakharov, *op. cit.*, p. 1011.

See also the report on the efforts of Sergei Batovrin to found a Soviet peace movement, in the *New York Times*, February 21, 1983. Mr. Batovrin's efforts have resulted in his internment in a Moscow psychiatric hospital; his group continues to be subject to severe harassment by Soviet authorities. Thus, our problem lies not with the Russian people—who may be presumed to desire peace as ardently as their Western counterparts—but with the Soviet regime.

Peace as a Political Weapon

by Vladimir Bukovsky

THE MAJOR PURPOSE of this paper will be to analyze developments during the past three years with regard to the European "peace movement" and the worldwide public debate on nuclear strategy, nuclear weapons, and related issues. Nearly three years ago, at the end of 1981, when the current upsurge of the "peace movement" had just begun, I became deeply worried by the one-sided presentation of the issues in question, by the irrational and hysterical reaction of many people who should have known better, and, above all, by the obvious Soviet manipulation of the "peace movement" which at the time nobody was willing to recognize.

This feeling of concern persuaded me to undertake a study of these problems and, by using Soviet sources open to the public, to demonstrate clearly the existence of Soviet involvement in the so-called European peace movement. As a result, I wrote a pamphlet entitled, *The Peace Movement and the Soviet Union*, which was published in part by the *Times* of London and later in its entirety by *Commentary*.[1] This pamphlet has also appeared in a number of European countries, and it has even been printed by an underground Polish publisher, Spotkania, under the title *Pacyfisci Kontra Pokoj*.

In view of the wide publicity this pamphlet has received, it seems pointless to repeat the same facts, arguments, and suggestions that were made more than two years ago. Instead, it will be much more valuable to analyze certain changes in the arguments of peace activists, changes that have been made in response to criticism, new political events, and shifts in the Kremlin's policies. Moreover, since the appearance of my pamphlet, there have been a number of new developments that should be included in the discussion of the Soviet role in the European "peace movement." We have seen a new round of Soviet-American talks on strategic and intermediate nuclear forces followed by a Soviet walkout, the continuing buildup of Soviet SS-20 missiles aimed against Western Europe, the initial deployment of Pershing II and cruise missiles by NATO in response to the SS-20 threat, and the emergence of independent peace movements in communist countries. Clearly, the nuclear debate has become much more sophisticated in the past year— despite, or because of, the Soviet decision to raise world tensions. Therefore,

---

[1] Vladimir Bukovsky, *The Peace Movement and the Soviet Union* (New York: Orwell Press, 1982); "Better Red than Dead is Not Good Enough," *Times* (London), December 4, 1981; "The Peace Movement and the Soviet Union," *Commentary*, May 1982. See, also, *Les Pacifistes contre la Paix* (Paris: Editione Robert Laffont, 1982); and *Pazifisten gegen den Frieden* (Bern, Switzerland: Verlag SOI, 1983). This pamphlet was also published in Sweden, the Netherlands, Denmark, Norway, Greece and Turkey, and reprinted in two collections of papers in the United States.

I feel it is necessary to update my pamphlet to include an analysis of the new political environment in which the European "peace movement" and its critics now find themselves.

The Struggle for Peace as a Soviet Foreign Policy Tool

First of all, let me briefly reiterate the main positions set forth in my pamphlet in 1981. Contrary to the allegations made by those who apparently did not read my pamphlet carefully, and yet have taken it upon themselves to criticize it, I did not ascribe the emergence of the peace movement in Europe to a "communist conspiracy." In fact, exactly the opposite is true: The "struggle for peace" has always been a cornerstone of Soviet foreign policy, a position openly proclaimed and inscribed in all Communist Party resolutions. According to Soviet ideology, real lasting peace can only be achieved by destroying capitalism, that "hotbed of contradictions and imperialist intentions." Why, they ask themselves, should brother-proletarians want to kill each other once they are free from "capitalist oppression"?

Moreover, according to their ideology, the ultimate triumph of communism in the world is historically inevitable, which means they do not need to initiate a world war unless they are certain they will win it. Of course, history must be encouraged and helped a bit now and then. Thus, a war fought in the "interests of the proletariat" is considered to be a "just war," because, they believe, it leads to the liberation of humanity from the "chains of capitalism," a development that will ultimately save mankind from the evils of war.

In practical terms, the "struggle for peace" has always been a useful tool of Soviet foreign policy. Communists have always known very well that the majority of the population in any country of the world would accept their rule only as a last resort—only when the alternative would be absolutely unbearable. They are, therefore, very skillful in exploiting unbearable situations (or in creating them, as in Poland), and they are extremely clever at molding political events to give the appearance that their rule is the only alternative. Thus, opponents appear to be "unreasonable" and "enemies of peace," while the communists are always "peacemakers."

Besides, in the ideological struggle it is much more advantageous to be on the side of such noble causes as "justice," "peace," "equality"—a terminological game played by the Soviets to the point of perfection. So, they are indeed "peace-lovers," if we are to accept their definition of peace.

One can find plenty of examples in recent history to confirm the consistency of the Soviets' "peaceful" policy as described above—the creation of the Soviet Union itself out of the ashes of World War I, the turmoil of the subsequent civil war, Moscow's "love affair" with Hitler, and the events during World War II. After the war they touted the cause of peace while trying to catch up with the West in the nuclear arms race and as a means to silence the public outcry over their occupation of Eastern Europe. And, now, as they try to retain their nuclear superiority over the West, they use it again to silence the growing criticism of Soviet adventurism in the Third World and of human rights violations at home. Finally, and perhaps most importantly, they exploit the cause of peace to extend their political influence in Western Europe. Once again a political foe of the Soviet Union—this time the Western democracies—is defamed as "unreasonable," as "insane," or as "warmongers" just because they do not want to accept the "lesser evil" of Soviet domination as an alternative to the ultimate evil of nuclear holocaust.

Also contrary to the hysterical outcry of many antinuclear activists, I did not imply in the 1981 pamphlet that the so-called peace movement consists exclusively of paid Soviet agents. In fact, I had taken the trouble to repeat at least four times within 50 pages that in my view the overwhelming majority of peace marchers are well-intentioned, albeit confused, naive, and frightened people. As usual, there are plenty of professional political profiteers who seek popularity by jumping on the bandwagon of peace at any price, just as there are plenty of people who try to exploit the atmosphere of panic for their own selfish purposes. But there is also not the slightest doubt that this motley crowd is manipulated by a handful of activists instructed directly from Moscow.

There were already quite a few facts available by the end of 1981 to prove the latter conclusion. To begin with, the peace movement's onesidedness itself was very revealing. The major constituent groups of the movement have conspicuously refrained from condemning Soviet imperialism in Afghanistan, Poland and other places, just as they have refused to denounce Soviet violations of international treaties and human rights agreements. They were crying shame on the Americans for merely planning to develop and deploy weapons like the enhanced radiation warhead and the cruise and Pershing missiles, but they were speaking only in whispers of the hundreds of Soviet SS-20s already aimed at Europe. They were happily throwing stones at General Haig in Germany, but Marshal Brezhnev did not provoke similar outbursts of anger.

There were, moreover, a number of reports on the heavy representation of communists in the leadership of the major peace groups, representation that was disproportional to their number in the rank-and-file. There were also occasional quarrels inside the peace movement over the existence of communist influence on decision-making, and there were even a few instances of direct Soviet involvement, as in the case of Arne Petersen in Denmark.

But most of the evidence of Soviet involvement in the European peace movement could easily be found by reading the Soviet newspapers and by comparing them with major peace movement publications. The new slogans adopted in Moscow would normally take from one to six months to migrate into major peace movement publications in Western Europe. The swiftness with which this occurred suggests a close, if somewhat indirect, link between some peace movement leaders and the masters of the Kremlin. The most striking example of West European peace activists following the Soviet lead was the designation of the last week in October as the target date for staging large peace rallies in Europe. This decision was first made public during the "World Parliament of Peoples for Peace" in Sofia, Bulgaria, in September 1980. Within a month, the first large antinuclear demonstrations took place in West European capitals.

It is also possible to trace the origin of the current peace campaign to specific Soviet actions. According to Soviet newspaper reports, the actual decision to begin supporting peace activists in the West was taken in the summer of 1979, more than a year before it was finally launched in Sofia. One can easily reconstruct the reasoning that led to this decision. If we keep in mind that since 1977 the Soviets have been deploying SS-20s at a rate of one per week, we should have no difficulty in realizing how helpful a peace movement in Western Europe could be in thwarting Western efforts to match the Soviet nuclear arms buildup in kind. There was, moreover, the need to preclude Western criticism of the Soviet invasion of Afghanistan, which was made about the same time the Kremlin decided to become involved in peace movements in the West. It was not difficult at the time for the Soviets to imagine what the West's reaction to these moves would be. It may mean the end of detente, they probably thought, but they knew that they could always resort to their traditional cold war strategy of combining provocations with the ever-present Soviet "struggle for peace."

The Peace Conference in Bulgaria

After a year of active preparations, the initial stages of the peace campaign were remarkably successful. The "peace conference" in Bulgaria in September 1980 attracted 2,260 delegates from 137 countries, who claimed to represent 330 political parties, 100 international associations, and over 3,000 national nongovernmental organizations. To be sure, this was no ordinary meeting of the international communist movement. The political spectrum of those represented was exceptionally wide: 200 members of different national parliaments, 200 trade-union leaders, 129 leading social democrats (33 of them members of their respective national executive bodies), 150 writers and poets, 33 representatives of different liberation movements, women's organizations, youth organizations, the World Council of Churches and other religious organizations, 18 representatives of different UN specialized committees, representatives of the Organization of

African Unity and of OPEC, retired military officers, and representatives of 83 communist parties.[2]

To gather such a wide variety of people from so many different political backgrounds to attend a political conference in a communist country is by no means an easy task. The possibility that their presence might be interpreted as an endorsement of the Soviet Union's aggressive and oppressive policies would normally deter many of them from coming. In the past even some communist parties would have hesitated to send their representatives. What happened on this occasion, however, was simply unbelievable: these 2,260 people voted unanimously to approve the absolutely pro-Soviet "Charter of the Peoples for Peace" and "Program for Action." How could this be possible in the wake of the Soviet occupation of Afghanistan, at a time when even many Western athletes had refused to participate in the Moscow Olympics?

Of course, one might guess that these "representatives" were quite carefully chosen in advance (after all, the Soviets had more than a year for preparations), and that only those known to be particularly "soft" on the peace issue were invited. Still, that alone could not have secured such a stunning success. To be sure, the gathering was convened not by the Soviet government or by a communist party, but by the World Peace Council. However, who does not know that this Council is a Soviet front organization? Moreover, the venue was carefully chosen—it was Bulgaria, not Czechoslovakia, or East Germany, let alone the Soviet Union. Still, who on earth could believe that Bulgaria would arrange an international conference independently from their Soviet masters.

The Soviet Use of the "Absolute Value"

The reason for the success of this conference is simply that the Soviets are extremely skilled at brainwashing people. One of their most successful tricks, the same one which is the very foundation of communist ideology, is to confront a human being with an "absolute value." Thus, the Soviets tout an absolute and everlasting happiness for mankind as an irresistibly appealing idea attainable only through communism. Similarly, the absolute and irreversible destruction of the entire globe, horrible as it is shown to be in numerous documentaries, is another "absolute value," only this time an absolutely negative one. Relativism is a difficult concept to grasp, let alone to live with. Absolute value, on the other hand, whether positive or negative, saves us from the spiritual anguish of having to choose constantly between good and better, between bad and worse. But it also deprives us of our free will. It enslaves us.

---

[2] *Pravda*, September 23-29, 1980; *Izvestia*, September 23-24, 27-28, 1980.

This subject is endless, and it is not my task here to plunge into an extended philosophical essay. But a comment is in order on the notorious decision by American Catholic bishops to declare that nuclear weapons are an absolute evil. Christian morality is a foundation of our civilization, and no one should think for a moment that the bishops have a monopoly on it. In my understanding, the Christian doctrine rejects simple arithmetic in the question of morality. Human life is proclaimed to be priceless, and one life is deemed to be as priceless as a dozen lives. Then, how can they calculate that nuclear war is immoral while conventional war is not? After all, the conventional World War II cost humanity some 50 million lives. Was it moral or immoral to defend ourselves against Hitler's aggression?

As I have pointed out earlier, the absolute value deprives us of free will, which is supposed to be given to us by God. As Sidney Hook quite rightly remarked, "Those who say that life is worth living at any cost have already written for themselves an epitaph of infamy, for there is no cause and no person that they will not betray to stay alive."[3] Indeed, such endorsement of immorality is very strange to hear from God's shepherds, who, after all, should be more concerned with a man's soul than with his survival.

Be that as it may, in practice it was precisely the psychological lure of the absolute value that lay behind the stunning success of Soviet propaganda in Sofia and elsewhere. In the name of the ultimate value, people were asked to betray their normal values. After sufficiently scaring them with the horrors of a possible nuclear holocaust, the Soviets warned them that the West was pushing the world toward the edge of catastrophe by imposing economic sanctions on the Eastern bloc and by boycotting cultural exchanges and sporting events (in response, of course, to the Soviet invasion of Afghanistan and the persecution of scientists in the USSR). In order to defuse the issue of human rights, which was clearly putting them on the defensive, the Soviets proclaimed a new slogan: "The people have the power to preserve peace—their main right." Thus, in pursuit of the ultimate right, the people were supposed to sacrifice all other rights. And they did. After all, who cares how many are arrested, tortured, or killed by the Soviets when the main task is to save humanity from destruction? Not surprisingly, nobody asked the Soviets the most obvious questions: "If you are so anxious to avoid holocaust, as you say, why should you continue to oppress your own people and others? Why should you remain in Afghanistan? Why should you not simply disarm unilaterally, as you require us to do?" No, nobody asked these questions, because the Soviets are known to be "impossible," while the West is known to be only "unreasonable" and often amenable to pressure.

Instead of asking the Soviets embarrassing questions, people of quite different professions have suddenly become preoccupied with the craft of

---

[3] *Los Angeles Times*, May 11, 1983.

diplomacy. They have been mesmerized by the "absolute value" and frightened by Soviet threats, deployment of SS-20s, and walkouts from arms reduction talks. Thus, American hosts of an official Soviet delegation are indignant when somebody tries to ask their guests an awkward question about violation of human rights or about persecution of Jews in the Soviet Union. Such questions are considered undiplomatic and detrimental to U.S.-Soviet relations. Justifying his decision to renew scientific exchanges with the Soviet Union at the very moment when Dr. Andrei Sakharov was reportedly dying in exile, the President of the American National Academy of Science, Frank Press, asserted: "Despite our continuous concern for Sakharov, there are some issues of such deep importance to the future of mankind that we have felt it necessary to continue talking about them with our Soviet counterparts. In this regard, arms control and international security are certainly of high priority. Our members feel very strongly about this issue."[4]

A respected scholar with no sympathy for communism, Professor John K. Galbraith, suddenly presents his readers with a highly optimistic view of the Soviet economy and goes even so far as to suggest that the Soviet people earn too much. Why?

I am not attracted by the Soviet system, but I am committed to the need of arms control—to the thought that after a nuclear exchange the ashes of communism will be indistinguishable from the ashes of capitalism, even by the most perceptive ideologist. But it is a prerequisite for the control of nuclear weapons that there be a modicum of confidence and trust between the two countries.[5]

Hence, on his recent "visit to Russia," he notices only similarities between the American and Soviet societies. He even gives his Soviet hosts advice on how to improve the image of communism:

When, in the Soviet Union, the spendable income exceeds the available supplies of the more sought-after goods, queues form at the shop. We saw these one day as we drove past a large shopping center on the edge of Leningrad. Standing in a queue is an uncomfortable thing; the shortages that induce it are seen as a failure of the government or the system. I asked my hosts if it wouldn't be wiser to distribute a little less income in relation to the supply of goods, since wages, after all, are under state control. In consequence, people would attribute their inability to buy to their failure to earn enough rather than to the failure of the economic system to supply the desired goods. Surely, that would be better for the reputation of the system."[6]

As for the question of nuclear disarmament, this "is an effort one pursues primarily at home."[7]

---

[4] *Washington Post*, May 11, 1984, p. A22.
[5] *The New Yorker*, September 3, 1984.
[6] *Ibid.*
[7] *Ibid.*

Soviet Influence over the Peace Movement

Once again, this time through the "peace movement," Soviet propaganda has managed to hoodwink a considerable number of people in the West. After taking a spiritual lead over the movement, it was not very difficult to take an organizational one. After all, if we are to accept the above philosophy, we must all unite irrespective of our past crimes, political differences, and beliefs in order to survive. That was precisely the message presented by the head of the Soviet "delegation," B. N. Ponomarev (Alternate Member of the Soviet Politburo and Head of the CPSU Central Committee's International Department), in a speech before the delegates to the Sofia conference. And it was accepted unanimously, not only by Soviet delegates, but by Westerners as well, by Catholic priests, social democrats, liberals, trade-unionists, and women's "lib" activists. For all our Western tolerance, is it still not shocking to see Westerners, no matter what their political cause, marching hand in hand with representatives of the Soviet Communist Party "to save humanity"?

What these multitudes of "inspired" people apparently do not know is that communists are incapable of normal human cooperation—they are either your enemies, or they rule you. It is necessary only to look at what happened to the Labour Party in Britain to understand this simple fact.[8] Thus, in no time the small and nearly forgotten European communist parties have taken over the leadership of the "peace movement" in Europe.

This fact has now, three years later, become common knowledge. In an article entitled, "The Story of Who's Behind Britain's CND,"[9] Douglas Eden reveals that there is a large proportion of members of the British Communist Party in the CND (Campaign for Nuclear Disarmament) conference leadership, and that even the resolutions of the CP's annual conferences are echoed by CND conference resolutions. More details of the communist manipulation of the CND are set forth in an excellent article by Alun Chalfont in *Encounter*, and similar facts concerning communist influence in the German and Dutch peace movements can be found in an article by Dr. Wynfred Joshua in *Strategic Review*.[10] The latter article also provides considerable

---

[8] The internal developments of the Labour Party are typical for any left-of-center political organization, especially in Europe (including the German Social Democratic Party): they are usually taken over by the left radicals and communists from within, unless they undergo a split. The scandals over the communist infiltration into the British Labour Party continued for several years, until the moderate part split off and formed the Social Democratic Party a few years ago. The Labour Party in Britain today is greatly influenced by its communist elements, and its 1984 platform includes unilateral nuclear disarmament, withdrawal from NATO, and a number of East European-type economic reforms.

[9] *Wall Street Journal*, February 22, 1983.

[10] Lord Chalfont, "The Great Unilateral Illusion," *Encounter*, 1983; and Wynfred Joshua, "Soviet Manipulation of the European Peace Movement," *Strategic Review*, Winter 1983.

information on the degree of direct Soviet involvement in the "peace movement" in the United States.

The evidence of direct Soviet involvement in the Western peace movement is so great that one could compile quite a lengthy catalog of facts and
references. For example, in Switzerland, where Novosti Press Agency officials were discovered to be running the entire peace movement, the Swiss
government closed the Bern bureau of Novosti, expelled the agency's bureau
chief, and forced the withdrawal of a Soviet diplomat it said was a KGB
officer responsible for overseeing Novosti's local operations. The Swiss
Foreign Ministry lodged a stiff formal protest with the Soviet Embassy ac-
cusing Novosti of "continued, grave interference in Swiss affairs incom-
patible" with its normal functions in a neutral country. The strongly word-
ed note and other official Swiss documents asserted that Novosti had been
involved in political activities ranging from masterminding antinuclear
demonstrations, organizing anti-American rallies, supervising one
demonstration that actually took place inside the chambers of the Swiss
Parliament, and purveying disinformation.[11]

While the Soviet escapade in Switzerland was handled firmly and con-
sistently by the Swiss government, American officials mishandled the issue
of Soviet influence in the U.S. "nuclear freeze" movement. Still suffering
from an anti-"McCarthyism" complex, the FBI Director promptly reassured
puzzled Americans that there was absolutely no evidence to suggest that
the Soviets were manipulating the American freeze movement, and this
line was quickly echoed by the "intelligence community." However, one
needs neither a community nor any great degree of intelligence to see that
the whole idea of a "nuclear freeze" originated in the Soviet Union, specifically with the personal appeal made in 1981 by the late President Brezhnev.
Apparently the local intelligence community does not read Brezhnev's
speeches; nevertheless, a community of even very low intelligence should
ask itself a very simple question: Why are Soviet proposals—from the
"verifiable freeze" to the "no-first-use" of nuclear weapons and the
"demilitarization of outer space"—always taken up by Western "peace
movements," while those forwarded by American and West European
governments are ignored and very often derided by the same groups?

Most importantly, the Soviets do not even attempt to conceal the fact
that they manipulate the "peace movements" in Western Europe. Indeed,
they openly admit that they have given them financial assistance. Thus,
in the February 1982 issue of an official Novosti Press Agency magazine,
Sputnik (published in English, French, German, and Russian, and available
in the bookshops of these countries), there appeared an editorial that ex-

---

[11] See John Vinocur, "West European Foes of New U.S. Missiles Often Find KGB Men in Their
Midst," *New York Times*, July 26, 1983; Associated Press Dispatch, April 29, 1983; and John Bar-
ron, "The KGB's Magical War for Peace," *Reader's Digest*, October 1982.

plained, with remarkable frankness, precisely what the purpose of the Soviet Peace Fund was: to give financial support to organizations, movements, and individuals who "struggle for peace and disarmament," and to sponsor international congresses, symposia, festivals, and exhibitions to give these organizations and individuals the opportunity to coordinate their activities on an international scale.

Later, on April 30, 1982, an article in *Pravda*, written by the head of the official Soviet Peace Committee, Yuri Zhukov (who is also a member of the CPSU's Central Committee), reported that the Soviet people enthusiastically contribute to the Soviet Peace Fund. According to Zhukov, over 80 million Soviet people had already made such contributions. Moreover, on May 31, 1982, *Pravda* reported that as of that date the Soviet people were obliged to donate one day's wages to the Soviet Peace Fund. The sum of money raised in this manner would be astronomical: the average one-day earning of a Soviet worker is five rubles; multiplying this by the number of "donors" indicated by Zhukov—80 million—means that 400,000,000 rubles would be available to the Soviet Peace Fund.

Clearly, some of the money is used inside the Soviet Union, as Yuri Zhukov informs us, to support 120 regional peace committees across the country. Still, if we were to assume that each regional committee employed, say, a maximum of 20 full-time employees (there are 19 employees at the headquarters of the Campaign for Nuclear Disarmament in Britain), we would have only a total of 2,400 full-time workers for the entire organization inside the Soviet Union. Multiplied by the annual earnings of the average Soviet worker, 2,000 rubles, this would amount to less than five million rubles as the total amount of money spent on wages by the Soviet Peace Fund inside the Soviet Union. Even if the expenses for travel, telephones, stationery, rents, and utilities were added to this amount, it would certainly not exceed 10 million rubles.

Let us suppose, then, that the Soviet Peace Fund sponsors trips for about 50,000 Western visitors to the Soviet Union per year. Let us also suppose that they receive royal treatment, the cost of which would unlikely be more than 5,000 rubles per trip. Even such an extremely generous estimate would account for only 250 million rubles. Adding the 10 million rubles which support the committees inside the Soviet Union gives us a total of 260 million rubles as a rough estimate of the accountable expenditures of the Soviet Peace Fund. Therefore, even if we were to compute a figure based on a minimum rate of donations and a maximum amount of expenses for internal activities, we would still be left with 140 million rubles to spend outside the Soviet Union, money to be used for sponsoring international congresses, conferences, festivals and exhibitions, and for supporting the activities of peace movements in the West. Even if this amount were converted into dollars using a "black market" rate of exchange, the Soviets would have available some \$35-\$45 million. The official rate of exchange would bring about \$233 million.

Finally, confirmation of the Soviet manipulation of the peace movement came from the leader of the European Nuclear Disarmament (END) organization himself, Professor E.P. Thompson. In a remarkable article, Thompson criticized his colleagues in the peace movement, calling them "sleepwalkers" who either do not see or refuse to worry about Soviet strategy toward the peace movement in the West.[12] As Thompson asserts: "The sleepwalkers in the peace movement can see no problem in all this. The United States intervenes continually in the West European political scene, and it is all a novelty to see the Soviet Union doing the same with success. And certain immediate Soviet aims run in the same direction as the aims of the peace movement. After all, they are quite as much against cruise missiles as is the most dedicated Western activist." He continues: " . . . alongside the Soviet peace offensive, clumsy attempts are now being made to split the Western peace movement and to bring it in line with Soviet strategies. There is now a busy traffic of meddlesome 'peace' brokers between East and West, mini-conferences (summoned by selective invitation) in Moscow, and preparations for a huge show-case 'Peace Assembly' in Prague."[13]

In another article, E.P. Thompson writes:

We do not stand in particular need of lessons from Yuri Zhukov, the President of the Soviet Peace Committee. Yet we have been receiving from him, and from several other sources in the Soviet Union and Eastern Europe, rather a lot of instructions in the past few months . . . . And Zhukov and his friends in the World Peace Council are trying in an old-fashioned 1950ish way to split our movement and bring it under the Soviet hegemony.

To the Russians, we are background music only, and music not even loud enough to swing a German election.

Our problems have been made worse in recent months by inept Soviet interventions in Western political life (including the peace movements) . . . .

We are willing to engage in discussions with official organizations over there, provided that the discussion is on honest and equal terms, and not on terms which coopt us into some pro-Soviet theatre of propaganda.[14]

What Has Changed in the Peace Movement?

Clearly, quotations from E.P. Thompson's articles indicate a sense of crisis in the West European "peace movement." What has happened?

---

[12] *Guardian*, February 21, 1983.
[13] *Ibid.*
[14] E.P. Thompson, "Peace and the East," *New Society*, June 2, 1983, pp. 349-352.

For one thing, a constant stream of criticism of the pro-Soviet orientation of peace movement propaganda has forced many antinuclear activists to become more critical of the Soviet Union. Peace movement leaders have not, for example, been able to continue their normal practice of excluding Soviet SS-20s from their usual condemnation of nuclear weapons. Nor have they been able to remain silent about Poland and Afghanistan.

At first, this criticism of Soviet policies and the SS-20s was tolerated by Moscow. As Soviet Peace Committee head Yuri Zhukov said, "What is our motto? No nuclear weapons in Europe—in East and West. No to nuclear weapons all over the world. We say we are against American missiles, Soviet missiles, French missiles, British missiles, and Chinese missiles. The bourgeois press totally conceals it."[15]

However, later, as criticism of the Soviet position increased in Western peace movements, the Soviets began to lose patience with the more impartial position taken by moderates. It became too dangerous. Thus, the peace movement may face the possibility of splitting between more pro-Soviet elements and more impartial ones.

As E. P. Thompson wrote in June 1983, "On one side, Yuri Zhukov and the operators of the World Peace Council accuse some of us of being 'anti-Soviet elements'; on the other side Michael Heseltine and Monsignor Bruno Heim accuse some of us of being 'useful idiots' and apologists for 'Soviet aggression.'"[16]

The first blow came with the imposition of martial law in Poland. As Thompson insists, quite correctly, "the unprecedented demonstrations [totaled] more than two million people in western European capitals in October and November 1981. And why were there not three million or four million demonstrating in the spring and summer of 1982? The answer is martial law in Poland and the repression of Solidarity."[17]

The second blow came from the Soviet position itself—the Soviet refusal to dismantle some of their SS-20s as a first step toward nuclear disarmament. The American "zero-option" proposal, the negotiations in Geneva, the more energetic propaganda of people committed to *multilateral* disarmament—all these developments have toned down the blatantly pro-Soviet position of many peace activists.

But the most devastating blow came with the persecution of the independent peace movements in Eastern Europe, primarily in East Germany and the Soviet Union. As 20 leaders of the American peace movement asserted in their letter to Brezhnev in September 1982:

---

[15] *Guardian*, April 14, 1983.
[16] Thompson, *op. cit.*
[17] *Ibid.*

84

The double standards by which the Soviet government abides—applauding widespread debate in the West, while crushing the most benign form of free expression at home—only strengthens the complex of forces that impel the nuclear arms race.

Renewed repression in the East, in particular of independent peace voices, will weaken Western peace movements and could—if they do not take precautions— paint them into an ineffectual "pro-Soviet" corner.[18]

In a similar vein, Thompson has asked:

But what can we do about it? To refuse to go to the conference [in Prague] might be seen as a refusal to "talk with the other side," which everyone now wants to do. To go might be seen as condoning the Soviet occupation of Czechoslovakia . . . as well as an acceptance of the repression of civil rights workers who have been trying to open a dialogue with the Western peace movement.

This question puts us at sixes and sevens and divided us more than any propaganda ploy by President Reagan could do.[19]

Despite these reservations, the European "peace movement" decided to send representatives to Prague, knowing full well that, according to Thompson, "the media in the West will expose us all, without discrimination, as Soviet stooges," and that "the event will do only harm to the cause of peace and will alienate democrats in the East from Western peace forces." He went on to say:

The principle of solidarity with unofficial and independent peace voices on the other side was endorsed by the majority of the multitude of peace organizations from Europe and the United States attending the Second European Nuclear Disarmament Convention in West Berlin last month [May]. Sadly, the official "peace committees" of the East boycotted the convention, while our independent friends in East Germany, Hungary, the Soviet Union and Czechoslovakia were refused exit visas to attend.[20]

Meanwhile, personal contacts between Western peace movement activists and leaders of the independent peace groups in the Eastern bloc were developed. Now, when taking their pilgrimages to Moscow, the Western peace movers have little excuse not to visit their counterparts. They inevitably witness the KGB persecution and the generally oppressive nature of the Soviet regime, and they slowly learn what I tried to explain to them two years ago in my pamphlet: that the internal oppressiveness and external aggressiveness of the Soviet regime are inseparable. They have suddenly learned that, as Thompson asserts, "Those weeping grandmothers, who

---

[18] *Ibid.*
[19] *Ibid.*
[20] *Ibid.*

still deck with flowers the graves of the last war, have dry eyes for Afghanistan, as they had, in 1968, for Czechoslovakia. The Soviet people will support their rulers in preparations for any war which is 'in defence of peace.'"[21] Finally, repeating almost word for word what I had written two years before, he states that "It is nonsense to try to extract something called 'the nuclear arms race' from the ideological and political context of which it is an integral part."[22]

The women who occupied Greenham Commons may still be a nuisance to the British government, but they have also become a problem for the Soviets. During their visit to Moscow in May 1983, they brought a member of an unofficial Russian peace group to an official meeting of the Soviet government's peace committee, thereby forcing Soviet officials to listen to a Russian dissident in an official forum.[23] Defending the arrested members of the Moscow independent peace group, the Greenham Commons women chided their hosts: "It is as easy to sit down in front of the Soviet Embassy as at the Greenham Commons."[24]

Clearly, the day when peace activists in the West refuse to march in demonstrations with communists, when this Soviet-inspired alliance is terminated, and when the crowds in European capitals demand the liberation of arrested peace activists in East Germany, the Soviet Union, Hungary, and Czechoslovakia as vigorously as they protest against nuclear weapons— that will be the day when the Soviets' political weapon of "peace" will turn against them.

Obviously, the Soviets realize the danger of losing control over the Western "peace movement." But what can they do? Expel all independent peace activists from the Soviet Union? If that were to happen, hundreds of thousands of Russians seeking an exit visa might then join the unofficial peace movement. Perhaps they will try to split the peace movement in the West, as Thompson believes they are now trying to do. But who knows how many peace activists would remain to support Moscow's policies—apart from communist comrades.

One thing is clear: Soviet leaders cannot allow an independent peace movement to flourish in the Soviet Union, or in any of the satellites either, for they simply cannot tolerate the existence of any politically independent movement within their borders. Now that their troops are in Afghanistan, this is even more true.

Nor can the Soviet Union allow the Western "peace movements" to split up, which is already happening in many countries. As a recent Moscow

---

[21] *Guardian*, February 21, 1983.
[22] *Ibid.*
[23] *Times*, May 27, 1983.
[24] *Ibid.*

shortwave radio report indicated, this became a major Soviet concern and a reason for calling a special Conference of Representatives of Anti-War Movements of Europe and North America in Helsinki in October 1984:

Special attention was given to a precise definition of the goals for the anti-war movement in its activity at the present stage. Many delegates, among them from the United States, Britain, Belgium and France, all belonging to different political trends, unanimously noted that the enemies of peace have devised sophisticated methods of undermining the anti-war movement, in a bid to force them off the course of the anti-missile and anti-nuclear struggle, and push some of them onto the road of revising the existing frontiers in Europe and meddling in the Socialist countries' internal affairs. Speakers at the conference exposed and denounced the maneuvers of those who seek to disunite the anti-war movement by dividing them into the so-called western and eastern groups. . . ."[25]

The Western Position

How well do Western politicians understand these new developments? Or, more precisely, how well do they understand that the questions of the arms race and disarmament do not exist outside the broader context of East-West relations? Do they understand that we are dealing with an ideological war that has very little to do with military hardware per se?

Judging by their behavior in the "nuclear debate," I would say that they do not understand it very well. Even leaving aside such questionable political actions as the recent Congressional approval of the nuclear freeze resolution, the current policy of the Western alliance in the nuclear debate is pathetic. It all consists of passive reactions to Soviet moves, proposals, and rhetorical exercises.

Of course, there were a few successes, such as President Reagan's "zero option" proposal, and a brilliant resolution passed by the United Nations in December 1982 protecting the right of individuals to organize peace movements.

But these timid steps in the right direction were never developed into a clear strategy for the West, although the need for, and the direction of, such a strategy were quite obvious. Once a mass political movement has come into being in a democratic country and is well-organized and well-financed, one cannot easily eliminate it. Nor should the legitimate concern of its supporters to avoid nuclear destruction be perceived as necessarily hostile to democracy. Indeed, a concerted effort should be made to prevent the manipulation of such a movement by a foreign power. A strategy should be devised to counter Soviet efforts to penetrate and dominate Western peace movements.

---

[25] Radio Moscow report by special correspondent Alexander Pagadin from Helsinki, Radio Moscow, North American Service (shortwave), October 8, 1984: 4:20, 6:20, 8:20, 9:20, and 11:20 p.m.

As the Soviets try to unite everyone behind their "peace" drives, our effort should be aimed at thwarting them by emphasizing the most controversial aspects of their campaign. Persecution of independent peace groups in communist countries and persistent Soviet violations of previous agreements should become targets of our counterattack. All confirmed facts of direct Soviet involvement with the peace movement in the West should be widely publicized. And, while the Soviets use the trick of the "absolute value," the "relative" horrors of communist rule should become a centerpiece of Western counterpropaganda, focusing on such graphic events as Soviet atrocities in Afghanistan, mass murder in Cambodia, and famine in Ethiopia. While the Soviets channel their funds through their most loyal groups within the peace movement, ways should be found to support more moderate groups.

But, most importantly, the issues of peace and the arms race should be returned to the natural context of East-West relations, with public attention being constantly redirected to Soviet intentions instead of the sheer amount of weapons accumulated by both sides. Paradoxically, the best Western position was formulated long before the peace movement became an issue. It is the Helsinki Accords, signed in 1975 by 35 countries of Europe, Canada and the United States, which links respect for human rights with the problems of security. All the West needed to counter the Soviet "peace" campaign of the past four years was to return to this formula, conveniently endorsed by the signatures of Brezhnev and other East European rulers. The logic of this position is impeccable: How can we control the arms race without verification, and how can we achieve verification without mutual trust? For that matter, how can anyone trust a government that does not allow its people to know the truth and discuss it and that deliberately instills hostility and hatred toward other nations into the minds of its population? How can we build trust with a nation whose citizens are not allowed to have a sincere and open dialogue with foreigners, under threat of imprisonment?

Those who may doubt the possible success of using this approach will be interested to know that the idea was tested in Los Angeles on June 5th, 1984, when the voters were offered the following proposition:

Shall the Los Angeles County Board of Supervisors transmit to the leaders of the United States and the Soviet Union a communication stating that the risk of nuclear war between the United States and the Soviet Union can be reduced if all people have the ability to express their opinions freely and without fear on world issues including the nations' arms policies; therefore, the people of Los Angeles County urge all nations that signed the Helsinki Accords on Human Rights to observe the Accords' provisions on freedom of speech, religion, press, assembly and emigration for all their citizens?

Despite vehement opposition by leaders of the nuclear freeze movement, the measure was carried by nearly a two-thirds majority.[26] Unfortunately, this idea has never been used on the national scale, let alone in the international arena.

Instead, U.S. leaders decided to begin arms reductions negotiations in Geneva—a big mistake, in my view. First of all, the idea of dragging the West into negotiations belongs to the Soviet strategists and represents for them a considerable victory. (See the resolution of the Soviet-sponsored World Parliament of Peoples for Peace, which, among other things, contains the demand: "Negotiate! There is no choice!"[27]) It is not difficult to understand why the Soviets badly needed to bring the United States into arms control negotiations: (a) they had been placed in political isolation by the invasion of Afghanistan, a plight that would be mitigated by arms negotiations; (b) SALT II had been rejected by the Senate; and (c) the West had finally awakened to discover that the Soviets had achieved strategic superiority, and Western leaders were about to engage in a new arms buildup.

Why did the West accept the Soviet call for arms control negotiations? It was clearly against Western interests because (a) it is always bad to accept the idea of the enemy, and (b) even worse to do so under the pressure of the Soviet-inspired peace movement; (c) arms negotiations with the Soviets is de facto justification of two major Soviet propaganda themes: that the danger of nuclear war is greater now than ever before (a position that works against Western efforts to match the Soviet arms buildup), and that the Western doctrine of nuclear deterrence does not work (and therefore does not need to be shored up by adding more nuclear weapons); (d) it is not wise to negotiate from a position of inferiority, as the West would be doing until its arms buildup is well along; (e) negotiations have reinforced the Soviet effort to focus the world's attention on the nuclear problem and away from Soviet aggression in Afghanistan and elsewhere; and (f) it amounted to acceptance of the dubious notion that it is possible to have mutually advantageous agreements with the Soviet Union, and that the Kremlin can be relied upon to abide by international agreements—despite the evidence on record, for example, the Helsinki Accords.

But more importantly, entering into arms negotiations with the Soviet Union means that the West has essentially accepted the Soviet proposition that the main threat in the world today comes from bombs and missiles and not from the Soviet system itself. In other words, it has amounted to an acceptance of the notion that disarmament can be discussed outside the context of East-West relations.

---

[26] *Wall Street Journal*, June 11, 1984, p. 22; and the *Washington Times*, June 8, 1984.
[27] *Pravda*, September 26, 1980.

All in all, it was an unbelievably inconsistent and irresponsible political decision. As a result, the United States has appeared to be weak, frightened, and under constant pressure. Once again, the Soviets have scored a propaganda victory and forced the West into a defensive position, and they did this at a time when they were vulnerable—at a time when they had been caught cheating on arms control agreements and the Helsinki Accords, and, above all, after having committed outright aggression in Afghanistan.

One can hardly perceive as an American victory the fact that the Soviets, overestimating their influence on world public opinion, did not force the West into further concessions when they walked out of the Geneva talks and deliberately increased international tensions. American foreign policy has become hostage to the idea of an inevitable arms control process, while tired Western societies are quite ready to return to the Soviet version of detente. It is a safe prediction that the Soviets will be more successful at the next stage of this vicious cycle.

Still worse, retreating further from what could be its position of advantage, the West seems to have accepted another Soviet idea and agreed to discuss "trust-building measures" with the Soviet Union separately from the issue of human rights. The Stockholm conference is probably the most vivid example of how little Western politicians understand about the nature of the problem they confront. I wonder what they discuss with the Soviets behind those closed doors in Stockholm: trust-building measures that are secret from the entire world but not from the Soviets? When the Helsinki Accords are so easily forgotten (without being officially repealed), who can trust any new treaty that may be concluded?

Instead of START or INF talks, the West should propose convening a conference to negotiate a postwar peace treaty in Europe, which to this day does not exist. Such a conference would allow us to concentrate on the real issues and the real threat to Western Europe and the United States, namely, the Soviet empire. Clearly, negotiating a peace treaty in Europe would be impossible without discussing Soviet postwar acquisitions and the occupation of Eastern Europe, without repealing the Hitler-Stalin Pact, and without discussing the unification of Germany and the withdrawal of foreign troops from European countries. This move would generate enormous pressure on the Soviets and force *them* onto the defensive.

Ideologically, the Soviet position would be untenable. They would not be able credibly to deny a referendum to countries occupied as a result of the Hitler-Stalin Pact while at the same time posing as a champion of European peace. In addition, focusing public attention on an all-European peace conference would most likely generate unrest in the already explosive areas of the Baltic states and the Western Ukraine. It would touch on the Soviet Union's most painful problem: the problem of nationalities.

Paradoxically, in such a conference the Soviet bloc would not be as monolithic as might be expected. Most of the East and Central European countries have numerous territorial claims on each other and on the Soviet Union, and the nationalistic feelings of all East Europeans would inevitably be stirred.

Given the current climate of peace hysteria, the Soviets could hardly refuse to participate in such a conference. Should they, nevertheless, refuse to attend, the burden of blame for the arms race, international tension, and the danger of nuclear holocaust would shift to the Kremlin, the crowds would move to our side, and Soviet influence over the Western peace movements would be lost.

Conclusion

Within a few years very little will be left of the "peace movement" in Europe. As soon as the new missiles are safely stationed, the current wave of aggressive pacifism will begin to subside. Most of these marchers will return to their usual pastimes: television, football, and the like. And nothing will penetrate their apathy.

Perhaps I will be the only one who will feel sorry because of it. For the first time in 30 years, the Soviets have handed us a powerful weapon which could have been turned against them to reverse the existing trend in international relations and neutralize the present source of danger in the world. Yet, through our lack of understanding and wisdom, we have failed to grasp the opportunity.

Thus, it seems that we will continue to squander billions of dollars in an endless arms race. We will continue to fight communism on the outskirts of our countries, but each time closer and closer to our homes. We will continue to deceive ourselves with the expectations that a "closet liberal" will somehow manage to make his way to the top of the Soviet ruling circles, or that the communist dictatorship will somehow be overthrown by a military coup. We will continue "business as usual" with Moscow—and hope for the best.

PERGAMON-BRASSEY'S
International Defense Publishers

List of Publications
in cooperation with the
Institute for Foreign Policy Analysis

Orders for the following titles should be addressed to: Pergamon-Brassey's, Maxwell House, Fairview Park, Elmsford, New York, 10523; or to Pergamon-Brassey's, Headington Hill Hall, Oxford, OX3 OBW, England.

Books

ATLANTIC COMMUNITY IN CRISIS: A REDEFINITION OF THE ATLANTIC RELATIONSHIP. Edited by Walter F. Hahn and Robert L. Pfaltzgraff, Jr. 1979. 386pp. $43.00.

REVISING U.S. MILITARY STRATEGY: TAILORING MEANS TO ENDS. By Jeffrey Record. 1984. 113pp. $16.95 ($9.95, paper).

INSTITUTE FOR FOREIGN POLICY ANALYSIS, INC.
List of Publications

Orders for the following titles in IFPA's series of Special Reports, Foreign Policy Reports, National Security Papers, Conference Reports, and Books should be addressed to the Circulation Manager, Institute for Foreign Policy Analysis, Central Plaza Building, Tenth Floor, 675 Massachusetts Avenue, Cambridge, Massachusetts 02139-3396. (Telephone: 617-492-2116.) Please send a check or money order for the correct amount together with your order.

Foreign Policy Reports

DEFENSE TECHNOLOGY AND THE ATLANTIC ALLIANCE: COMPETITION OR COLLABORATION? By Frank T. J. Bray and Michael Moodie. April 1977. 42pp. $5.00.

IRAN'S QUEST FOR SECURITY: U.S. ARMS TRANSFERS AND THE NUCLEAR OPTION. By Alvin J. Cottrell and James E. Dougherty. May 1977. 59pp. $5.00.

ETHIOPIA, THE HORN OF AFRICA, AND U.S. POLICY. By John H. Spencer. September 1977. 69pp. $5.00. (Out of print).

BEYOND THE ARAB–ISRAELI SETTLEMENT: NEW DIRECTIONS FOR U.S. POLICY IN THE MIDDLE EAST. By R. K. Ramazani. September 1977. 69pp. $5.00.

SPAIN, THE MONARCHY AND THE ATLANTIC COMMUNITY. By David C. Jordan. June 1979. 55pp. $5.00.

U.S. STRATEGY AT THE CROSSROADS: TWO VIEWS. By Robert J. Hanks and Jeffrey Record. July 1982. 69pp. $7.50.

THE U.S. MILITARY PRESENCE IN THE MIDDLE EAST: PROBLEMS AND PROSPECTS. By Robert J. Hanks. December 1982. vii, 77pp. $7.50.

SOUTHERN AFRICA AND WESTERN SECURITY. By Robert J. Hanks. August 1983. 71pp. $7.50.

THE WEST GERMAN PEACE MOVEMENT AND THE NATIONAL QUESTION. By Kim R. Holmes. March 1984. 73pp. $7.50.

THE HISTORY AND IMPACT OF MARXIST-LENINIST ORGANIZATIONAL THEORY. By John P. Roche. April 1984. 73pp. $7.50.

Special Reports

THE CRUISE MISSILE: BARGAINING CHIP OR DEFENSE BARGAIN? By Robert L. Pfaltzgraff, Jr., and Jacquelyn K. Davis. January 1977. x, 53pp. $3.00.

EUROCOMMUNISM AND THE ATLANTIC ALLIANCE. By James E. Dougherty and Diane K. Pfaltzgraff. January 1977. xiv, 66pp. $3.00.

THE NEUTRON BOMB: POLITICAL, TECHNICAL AND MILITARY ISSUES. By S.T. Cohen. November 1978. xii, 95pp. $6.50.

SALT II AND U.S. STRATEGIC FORCES. By Jacquelyn K. Davis, Patrick J. Friel and Robert L. Pfaltzgraff, Jr. June 1979. xii, 51pp. $5.00.

THE EMERGING STRATEGIC ENVIRONMENT: IMPLICATIONS FOR BALLISTIC MISSILE DEFENSE. By Leon Gouré, William G. Hyland and Colin S. Gray. December 1979. xi, 75pp. $6.50.

THE SOVIET UNION AND BALLISTIC MISSILE DEFENSE. By Jacquelyn K. Davis, Uri Ra'anan, Robert L. Pfaltzgraff, Jr., Michael J. Deane and John M. Collins. March 1980. xi, 71pp. $6.50. (Out of print).

ENERGY ISSUES AND ALLIANCE RELATIONSHIPS: THE UNITED STATES, WESTERN EUROPE AND JAPAN. By Robert L. Pfaltzgraff, Jr. April 1980. xii, 71pp. $6.50.

U.S. STRATEGIC-NUCLEAR POLICY AND BALLISTIC MISSILE DEFENSE: THE 1980s AND BEYOND. By William Schneider, Jr., Donald G. Brennan, William A. Davis, Jr., and Hans Rühle. April 1980. xii, 61pp. $6.50.

THE UNNOTICED CHALLENGE: SOVIET MARITIME STRATEGY AND THE GLOBAL CHOKE POINTS. By Robert J. Hanks. August 1980. xi, 66pp. $6.50.

FORCE REDUCTIONS IN EUROPE: STARTING OVER. By Jeffrey Record. October 1980. xi, 92pp. $6.50.

SALT II AND AMERICAN SECURITY. By Gordon J. Humphrey, William R. Van Cleave, Jeffrey Record, William H. Kincade, and Richard Perle. October 1980. xvi, 65pp.

THE FUTURE OF U.S. LAND-BASED STRATEGIC FORCES. By Jake Garn, J. I. Coffey, Lord Chalfont, and Ellery B. Block. December 1980. xvi, 80pp.

THE CAPE ROUTE: IMPERILED WESTERN LIFELINE. By Robert J. Hanks. February 1981. xi, 80pp. $6.50. (Hardcover, $10.00).

THE RAPID DEPLOYMENT FORCE AND U.S. MILITARY INTERVENTION IN THE PERSIAN GULF. By Jeffrey Record. February 1981. viii, 82pp. $7.50. (Hardcover, $12.00).

POWER PROJECTION AND THE LONG-RANGE COMBAT AIRCRAFT: MISSIONS, CAPABILITIES AND ALTERNATIVE DESIGNS. By Jacquelyn K. Davis and Robert L. Pfaltzgraff, Jr. June 1981. ix, 37pp. $6.50.

THE PACIFIC FAR EAST: ENDANGERED AMERICAN STRATEGIC POSITION. By Robert J. Hanks. October 1981. ix, 75pp. $7.50.

NATO's THEATER NUCLEAR FORCE MODERNIZATION PROGRAM: THE REAL ISSUES. By Jeffrey Record. November 1981. vii, 102pp. $7.50.

THE CHEMISTRY OF DEFEAT: ASYMMETRIES IN U.S. AND SOVIET CHEMICAL WARFARE POSTURES. By Amoretta M. Hoeber. December 1981. xiii, 91pp. $6.50.

THE HORN OF AFRICA: A MAP OF POLITICAL-STRATEGIC CONFLICT. By James E. Dougherty. April 1982. xv, 74pp. $7.50.

THE WEST, JAPAN AND CAPE ROUTE IMPORTS: THE OIL AND NON-FUEL MINERAL TRADES. By Charles Perry. June 1982. xiv, 88pp. $7.50.

THE GREENS OF WEST GERMANY: ORIGINS, STRATEGIES, AND TRANSATLANTIC IMPLICATIONS. By Robert L. Pfaltzgraff, Jr., Kim R. Holmes, Clay Clemens, and Werner Kaltefleiter. August 1983. xi, 105pp. $7.50.

THE ATLANTIC ALLIANCE AND U.S. GLOBAL STRATEGY. By Jacquelyn K. Davis and Robert L. Pfaltzgraff, Jr. September 1983. viii, 44pp. $7.50.

WORLD ENERGY SUPPLY AND INTERNATIONAL SECURITY. By Herman Franssen, John P. Hardt, Jacquelyn K. Davis, Robert J. Hanks, Charles Perry, Robert L. Pfaltzgraff, Jr., and Jeffrey Record. October 1983. xiv, 93pp. $7.50.

POISONING ARMS CONTROL: THE SOVIET UNION AND CHEMICAL/BIOLOGICAL WEAPONS. By Mark C. Storella. June 1984. xi, 99pp. $7.50.

National Security Papers

CBW: THE POOR MAN'S ATOMIC BOMB. By Neil C. Livingstone and Joseph D. Douglass, Jr., with a Foreword by Senator John Tower. February 1984. x, 33pp. $5.00.

Books

SOVIET MILITARY STRATEGY IN EUROPE. By Joseph D. Douglass, Jr. Pergamon Press, 1980. 252pp. (Out of print).

THE WARSAW PACT: ARMS, DOCTRINE, AND STRATEGY. By William J. Lewis. New York: McGraw-Hill Publishing Co., 1982. 471pp. $29.95.

THE BISHOPS AND NUCLEAR WEAPONS: THE CATHOLIC PASTORAL LETTER ON WAR AND PEACE. By James E. Dougherty. Archon Books, 1984. 255pp. $22.50.

Conference Reports

NATO AND ITS FUTURE: A GERMAN-AMERICAN ROUNDTABLE. Summary of a Dialogue. 1978. 22pp. $1.00.

SECOND GERMAN-AMERICAN ROUNDTABLE ON NATO: THE THEATER-NUCLEAR BALANCE. A Conference Report. 1978. 32pp. $1.00.

THE SOVIET UNION AND BALLISTIC MISSILE DEFENSE. A Conference Report. 1978. 26pp. $1.00.

U.S. STRATEGIC-NUCLEAR POLICY AND BALLISTIC MISSILE DEFENSE: THE 1980S AND BEYOND. A Conference Report. 1979. 30pp. $1.00.

SALT II AND AMERICAN SECURITY. A Conference Report. 1979. 39pp.

THE FUTURE OF U.S. LAND-BASED STRATEGIC FORCES. A Conference Report. 1979. 32pp.

THE FUTURE OF NUCLEAR POWER. A Conference Report. 1980. 48pp. $1.00.

THIRD GERMAN-AMERICAN ROUNDTABLE ON NATO: MUTUAL AND BALANCED FORCE REDUCTIONS IN EUROPE. A Conference Report. 1980. 27pp. $1.00.

FOURTH GERMAN-AMERICAN ROUNDTABLE ON NATO: NATO MODERNIZATION AND EURO-PEAN SECURITY. A Conference Report. 1981. 15pp. $1.00.

SECOND ANGLO-AMERICAN SYMPOSIUM ON DETERRENCE AND EUROPEAN SECURITY. A Conference Report. 1981. 25pp. $1.00.

THE U.S. DEFENSE MOBILIZATION INFRASTRUCTURE: PROBLEMS AND PRIORITIES. A Conference Report (The Tenth Annual Conference, sponsored by the International Security Studies Program, The Fletcher School of Law and Diplomacy, Tufts University). 1981. 25pp. $1.00.

U.S. STRATEGIC DOCTRINE FOR THE 1980s. A Conference Report. 1982. 14pp.

FRENCH-AMERICAN SYMPOSIUM ON STRATEGY, DETERRENCE AND EUROPEAN SECURITY. A Conference Report. 1982. 14pp. $1.00.

FIFTH GERMAN-AMERICAN ROUNDTABLE ON NATO: THE CHANGING CONTEXT OF THE EURO-PEAN SECURITY DEBATE. Summary of a Transatlantic Dialogue. A Conference Report. 1982. 22pp. $1.00.

ENERGY SECURITY AND THE FUTURE OF NUCLEAR POWER. A Conference Report. 1982. 39pp. $2.50.

INTERNATIONAL SECURITY DIMENSIONS OF SPACE. A Conference Report (The Eleventh Annual Conference, sponsored by the International Security Studies Program, The Fletcher School of Law and Diplomacy, Tufts University). 1982. 24pp. $2.50.

PORTUGAL, SPAIN AND TRANSATLANTIC RELATIONS. Summary of a Transatlantic Dialogue. A Conference Report. 1983. 18pp. $2.50.

JAPANESE-AMERICAN SYMPOSIUM ON REDUCING STRATEGIC MINERALS VULNERABILITIES: CURRENT PLANS, PRIORITIES AND POSSIBILITIES FOR COOPERATION. A Conference Report. 1983. 31pp. $2.50.

NATIONAL SECURITY POLICY: THE DECISION-MAKING PROCESS. A Conference Report (The Twelfth Annual Conference, sponsored by the International Security Studies Program, The Fletcher School of Law and Diplomacy, Tufts University). 1983. 28pp. $2.50.

THE SECURITY OF THE ATLANTIC, IBERIAN AND NORTH AFRICAN REGIONS. Summary of a Transatlantic Dialogue. A Conference Report. 1983. 25pp. $2.50.

THE WEST EUROPEAN ANTINUCLEAR PROTEST MOVEMENT: IMPLICATIONS FOR WESTERN SECURITY. Summary of a Transatlantic Dialogue. A Conference Report. 1984. 21pp. $2.50.

THE U.S.-JAPANESE SECURITY RELATIONSHIP IN TRANSITION. Summary of a Transpacific Dialogue. A Conference Report. 1984. 23pp. $2.50.

SIXTH GERMAN-AMERICAN ROUNDTABLE ON NATO: NATO AND EUROPEAN SECURITY— BEYOND INF. Summary of a Transatlantic Dialogue. A Conference Report. 1984. 31pp. $2.50.

SECURITY COMMITMENTS AND CAPABILITIES: ELEMENTS OF AN AMERICAN GLOBAL STRATEGY. A Conference Report (The Thirteenth Annual Conference, sponsored by the International Security Studies Program, The Fletcher School of Law and Diplomacy, Tufts University). 1984. 21pp. $2.50.

THIRD JAPANESE-AMERICAN-GERMAN CONFERENCE ON THE FUTURE OF NUCLEAR ENERGY. A Conference Report. 1984. 40pp. $2.50.

95